†30.00

CRANBROOK

A Wealden Town

C. C. R. PILE

with a foreword by

V. SACKVILLE-WEST

**CRANBROOK AND SISSINGHURST
LOCAL HISTORY SOCIETY**
1955

EAGLE PRINTING WORKS
Cranbrook, Kent

CONTENTS

FOREWORD: V. SACKVILLE-WEST

CONTENTS

ILLUSTRATIONS

FOREWORD

Although I have now lived within three miles of Cranbrook for a quarter of a century, I never knew much about it before reading Mr. Pile's most informative book. True, I had always thought of Cranbrook as a small epitome of Kentish History, a conception now amply confirmed by the painstaking and scholarly researches embodied in the following pages. The outlines were already familiar: the dark forest, the droves of swine, the few clearings or denes, with their still living evidence in the suffix *den* in so many of our place-names; the coming of the Romans, the straight drive of the Roman roads cutting through the forest in the stern Roman way; then the departure of the Romans, abandoning Britain after four hundred years of civilising occupation, leaving traces near Cranbrook of a villa or homestead, the tiles still blackened by soot almost two thousand years old, and scattered evidence of other villas near Frittenden, all suggesting that these Italians had settled themselves very comfortably in this conquered island so long as they remained established with their wives and families. Unfortunately for us, they went away, leaving the native inhabitants to get on as best they could for themselves.

The native inhabitants did very well. As we come down through the centuries, we find the development of the wool trade: Cranbrook streets must metaphorically have been noisy with the bleating of sheep. Cranbrook's houses must likewise have echoed to the blows of the hammer on iron for smelting. Cranbrook was becoming prosperous. Queen Elizabeth I honoured our town with a visit. Her citizens started going off in the great adventure of the New World, and to this day there is a Cranbrook near Detroit which retains a warm feeling for its home-town in Kent. I remember myself, meeting a Mr. Chittenden somewhere in the U.S.A., a large, broad-shouldered man who bore down on me and described what he called a pilgrimage to Cranbrook, the place of origin of his ancestors, generously rewarded by finding his own name written above a grocer's shop. "Say, Miss Sackville-West, you wouldn't credit what a thrill that gave me."

Such is the continuity of our history.

Mr. Pile has now come nobly forward, to fill in the outlines with a mass of detail, factual and chronological, lovingly drawn from the old records. A severe historian and archæologist, he has not said very much about the charm of the little town ; perhaps he did not consider such frivolities as coming within the terms of his self-appointed function, or perhaps he thought that that would be better left to me, as an ignorant but appreciative observer of the picturesque. So I may allow myself to add a word in praise of Cranbrook, dominated as it is by its old windmill, its really beautiful church and church-yard planted with magnolias and flowering trees ; its narrow street, inconvenient for present-day traffic ; its wider street, and the many old houses such as the one called The Abbey ; its air of busy peace on a shopping day. I have often thought that if I wanted to show an over-seas visitor a sample of a small and very English country town, I need not go further afield than my three-mile distant Cranbrook, with its legacy of history behind it.

V. SACKVILLE-WEST.

Sissinghurst Castle.

CRANBROOK

A Wealden Town

CHAPTER I

THE GREAT FOREST

" Old Andredsweald at length doth take her time to tell,
The changes of the world, that since her youth befell
When yet upon her soil scarce human feet had trode ;
A place where only then the Sylvans made abode."

There is a general agreement that the name of Cranbrook
is derived from CRAN = a crane or heron (or possibly a
personal name) and BROC = a stream or marshy place.
Whether this is correct, or whether the Crane stream does in
fact take its name from the parish in which it rises is a matter
not easily to be resolved, but it may be assumed, whatever the
derivation, that the origin of the name is Old English ; this
assumption leads to the conclusion that the earliest settlement
of the parish occurred during the Saxon days. The name of
Cranbrook or Cranbroca has not been traced in any document
earlier than the end of the eleventh century, but other
evidence, which is discussed later, suggests the earliest
permanent settlements in the parish may have been established
before the ninth century, the absence of any indications
of permanent habitation before this date must not be allowed
to create the impression that the area was a dreary expanse
of forest, scrub and swamp.

The forest of Andred, extending for more than 120 miles
over the width of the modern counties of Kent, Sussex and
Hampshire, formed a part of the primeval wood that covered
much of England, although it can seldom have been a
continuous expanse of heavy timber ; it furnished the early
inhabitants, settled near the coast or on the high ground, with
their timber, and on occasion offered a place of refuge for
them from their enemies. Deep in the heart of this great
forest stood the site that in good time would see the early

settlements that were to be the foundations of the modern parish of Cranbrook.

Sufficient evidence has been obtained to suggest that the district was peopled in the Bronze Age; flint implements of this period have been discovered in the field at the top of Windmill Hill, arrowheads at Colliers Green and Golford, a flint knife near the Common and another at Farningham, to mention only a few. The only known settlement of this pre-Roman period lies just outside the parish at Knox Bridge, where there is an example of a moated stronghold. This has a circumference of roughly 300 yards, and is situated within a few feet of the stream from which it could be filled. When the moat was cleared out in the middle of the last century many of the stump ends of trees were found with which the inner edge had been palisaded round, as described by Caesar. The interior is bowl shaped and symmetrical. Entrance was by a bridge of planks which could be destoyed in case of need. A similar earthwork in the same field was destroyed about 1850.

Although it is known that the iron deposits in the forest were worked as early as 100 B.C. in East Sussex, between Sedlescombe and Brede, no traces of iron being worked at this period have been found in the neighbourhood of Cranbrook.

Caesar landed in Britain in the year 55 B.C., although it was not until A.D. 46 that the Romans occupied the country and brought it under their control, Kent becoming part of a peaceful province of the Empire. In Cranbrook there may be found traces of road, built towards the end of the third century; this highway was not a main military road but a north-south crossing of the Weald constructed for commercial reasons in order to link the Rochester and Maidstone district with the Sussex ironworks; from Staplehurst to the foot of Camden Hill it follows the line of the modern highway—it has next been traced in the street at Sissinghurst near the Bull, from whence it crosses Chapel Lane (where a section has been exposed for its full width) and on to the crossroads at Golford. Leaving the new Benenden road to the east it runs parallel for a short distance with the stream called the Ommenden as far as the old Mill Pond at Chittenden, continuing on to the park at Hemsted; here it divided with the main track passing over the Roman Ford between Benenden and Iden Green, through Sandhurst and so to Bodiam, the other branch turning eastward and leading to Ashford.

There is a widely held view that the Weald remained completely uninhabited during the whole period of the Roman occupation, but there are indications that may cause this opinion to be modified. Roman tiles and burial urns were found at Frittenden during the last century, and at a later date tiles and pottery were reported from Smarden. Recently many pieces of broken roof and floor tiles together with numerous portions of box flue tiles crosscut for keying to plaster were recovered from a field on Little Farningham Farm, Cranbrook, close to the line of the Roman road.

A few fragments of pottery were also recovered and much iron slag, which may have been moved from the road when the field was ploughed. Until the site has been more thoroughly explored by a trial trench it is naturally impossible to estimate the importance of these discoveries, but first impressions suggest the possibility of a building of the 3rd or 4th centuries, having some connection with the Roman Navy, many of the tiles being stamped with the inscription CL. BR. (Classis Britannia).

The majority of the inhabitants of Roman Britain lived in the country either in the villages or in isolated farmhouses. These latter, usually referred to as villas whether large or small, stood in the midst of their own lands away from the villages ; they were self-supporting and usually Romanized, often with hypocausts. Such farms were not uncommon even in pre-Roman days, and their occupants by degrees acquired Roman ways of living, improving their dwellings until they became villas of the Roman type.

It is not without interest to note that a gold finger ring of a British or Celtic pre-Roman type was ploughed up in a field on Bettenham Farm in 1868 ; there may have been scattered settlers in the Weald at an earlier period than has hitherto been thought likely.

Most of the isolated villas were farms, but there have been exceptional cases recorded where an industry such as tile making or iron working was carried on. The iron workings in Sussex were already active many years before the Romans landed in Britain ; during the occupation their importance increased to an extent sufficient to justify the construction of the road already mentioned. It is probable that a careful investigation of the area adjoining the line of the road through the Weald might reveal further evidence of more settlements.

CHAPTER II

THE DENES

" England shall bide till Judgment Tide
By Oak, and Ash, and Thorn."

—Kipling.

When the Romans withdrew their troops in 410, they left a country that had enjoyed for many years all the privileges and benefits of the Empire. The Christian faith had been introduced and embraced by a large number of the inhabitants, whilst the civilizing influence of Rome was evident on every hand. In the years that immediately followed the withdrawal, little change could be observed, but gradually the pressure from enemies beyond the defenceless frontiers started a process of disruption and destruction.

The first invasion by the men who crossed the North Sea in 449 marked the beginning of a new chapter. Kent was occupied by the Jutes, who probably came from the area around the mouth of the Rhine. They landed to find the country closely related to the Frankish Rhineland in culture, something not to be found in other parts of England. Little is known of the history of the next hundred years, nor can the fate of the inhabitants be determined, they may have been absorbed by their conquerors, or have been slowly forced westwards.

Sir Frank Stenton (" Anglo-Saxon England ") states that the local names of the Kentish Weald are in general of an ancient type and prove that the intricacies of these regions had been familiar from a very early time. Before the 8th century the only kind of territorial unit less than an entire kingdom was vaguely referred to by historians of the period as a region, and in Kent these early divisions ultimately developed into the Lathes.

The Weald served as a great reserve of swine pasture for the use of communities living in the more open part of the country. At first these woodlands were divided between a small number of large " folks " or regions and used in accordance with their ancient customs. The names Limenweara wald and Weowara wald recorded early in the 8th century proved that the woodlands to which they applied were then regarded as belonging to those regions or " folks " which afterwards appear as the Lathes of Lyminge and Wye.

Up to this moment it is doubtful if there was any real question of ownership of the Weald, other than by the community at large, but early in the 9th century the Kings of Kent began the process by which the ancient stretches of pasture for swine were divided into separate blocks and assigned to individual owners. The Old English name for these pasturages for swine is " Denbera " and thus they came to be referred to in the later charters as dens or denes, even although the actual place was called " hurst," " ley," " ridge " or other suffix. These early transfers of land were gifts rather than grants, and empowered the recipient to take the dues and services that the local inhabitants had formerly rendered to the King.

The early charters, many of which were grants to the Monastic Foundations, often contained a phrase that implied the grant to be by the King with the approval of the people, confirming the suggestion of common ownership, but later ones omit a clause that would appear to question the power of the King to make a grant in his own right.

These 9th century charters furnish the earliest records of some of the denes which were eventually to form the parish of Cranbrook.

These denes, known by distinct names, were attached to estates in the more populous parts of the county, and although the name of manor had not yet come into use, there was a definite tendency towards an economy of a manorial kind, and the later unusual manorial economy of the Weald could not have arisen without this background of the forest denes.

The earliest of charters from which it is possible to identify particular denes bears the date 804, when the Abbot of St. Augustine's was granted Lenham and twelve denes bearing acorns in the Weald, including Plussinghert (now Flissinghurst), Cumbdene (Camden) and Frydreleah (possibly Friezley).

In 814, Coenwulf, King of Mercia, granted a certain dene called Begegebyra (Bedgbury).

Little Chart, purchased by the Archbishop of Canterbury and given by him to the Monastery of Christ Church in 843, included the denes of Cadaca Hrych or Karkeregge (part of the later hamlet of Milkhouse) and Heoratleagh (Hartley).

A few years earlier, in 822, Beornulfus, King of Mercia, had given Godmersham to Christ Church, this included certain denes in the Weald, although they are not named, there is a presumption that they included the denes of Cranbroke and Thornden (Turnden), for at a much later date those denes are referred to as part of the manor of Godmersham.

There are many more similar references, enough has been quoted to justify the assumption that by the end of the 10th century the outline of the modern parish of Cranbrook had already begun to take form. All these denes, and many more, had been partially settled ; cultivation of cleared spaces in the woods assured a local supply of food, and although each dene would tend to turn to the manor or estate on which it was dependent for many things, the local interests of these scattered settlements were slowly creating a new community in the heart of the forest. There is no direct evidence that gives any indication of the date of the first church built for the needs of this young community. It was a custom to erect a tall wooden cross in a convenient place for a daily service of prayer in those districts that had not a more permanent place of worship, and it may well have been the case at Cranbrook.

But there are reasons for supposing that a church of wood and thatched with brushwood had been built early in the 11th century, probably by Christ Church, the owners of the denes of Cranbrook, Hartley (part) and Thornden, as well as Sissinghurst and Bettenham to the east, for many new churches were arising on the manorial estates of the church at this period.

Although the earliest records of the denes only date back to the commencement of the ninth century, their history starts many years earlier than this. At this time the forest had long been used as pasturage for the herds of swine that figured so prominently in the economy of Saxon estates. At first these herds were fed in certain undefined areas, but with the increase in their numbers it became necessary to deliminate the area within which they must be restricted, and thus the boundaries of each dene came to be set out. There followed the partial clearing of a piece of the forest in those denes where the swineherds had become permanent settlers,

14

living in wattle and thatch huts and cultivating the land adjoining.

These denes continually recur in the later history of those manors with interests in Cranbrook—most of their names are still in current use.

CHAPTER III

1066 AND AFTER

" Stubborn all were his people, a stark and jealous horde,
Not to be schooled by the cudgel, scarce to be cowed by
the sword,

Blithe to turn at their pleasure, bitter to cross in their mood,
And set on the ways of their choosing, as the hogs of
Andred's wood."

—" Traffic and Discoveries," Kipling.

When William of Normandy defeated Harold at Senlac in 1066 the victory amounted to more than a battle won ; it marked, as everyone knows, a turning point in history. A small aristocracy replaced the old English nobility and soon obtained control, not only of the posts of responsibility at the Court, but of local and rural government as well. Yet in many forms of culture the English were the superior of their conquerors ; they had great respect for the law and their courts of justice, a sound currency based on their silver penny, some of the best craftsmen in Europe, and a system of taxation on a national basis. The Normans excelled in the art of warfare, and not all the bravery of the English, fighting on foot, could prevail over the superior skill in the use of the sword and lance that their mounted opponents displayed.

Yet for the humble peasants and herdsmen dwelling in the Wealden forest clearings, little difference would be apparent. Most of the land on which they dwelt belonged to the Church, and when the Conqueror granted his followers their estates in the newly won country, the property of the Church was left untouched for the most part. Wye, a manor of the English Kings, passed to the newly founded abbey at Battle, with its appendant denes, which included those of Angley and Winesley (Willesley), both in the future parish of Cranbrook.

Queen Edith, sister of Harold and wife of Edward the Confessor, owned the dene of Badlingden from the manor of Hadlow, which went to Odo. Harold himself held the Denes of Gordene and Trenley as of the manor of Boughton Aluph, which was granted to Eustace of Boulogne. Sinketweasle, Swatlinden, Rodelinden and Critholl were other denes in lay ownership.

It is often averred that no mention of Cranbrook can be found in the Domesday book, and in so far as the actual name of Cranbrook is concerned this is so.

There is no record of a church either, but this gives no ground for the assumption that none existed at this time.

The Commissioners who carried out the Domesday Survey assumed, in the first place, that all the land in England could be assigned to residences of persons of a higher rank than the mass of the population. The French word " manoir " was the word a foreign clerk would employ to denote an estate or economic unit not unfamiliar to the Englishmen of pre-Conquest England.

Manor (the word merely means house) is a vague expression used to describe a large variety of estates ; some were compact units, but others included parcels of woodland or marsh lying far distant from the house and centre of the estate.

When the Domesday Survey was made, most of the county had long been organized into Hundreds and Lathes, but this was not the case with the Weald. Any information it contains about this district must be looked for under the manors to which the many denes were attached. Unfortunately, the Commissioners were not required to give precise details of the property they were entering in their register, and so it is found that most of the entries relating to the manors holding land in the Weald merely state " pannage for 200 hogs " or " wood for the pannage of 20 hogs " or " three denes," it is only by following up the later history of the manors that it becomes possible to identify with reasonable certainty the names of these denes.

Briefly then, the Domesday Survey presented a list of all the chief landowners in the county, followed by a description of the estates each tenant-in-chief held in the county. There were no manors in Cranbrook at the time, the church was not manorial and thus there is no mention of the name in the Survey. This absence of direct information applies to most of the Weald for the reasons already stated despite the evidence of fairly general settlement in the area.

The records of the next hundred years or more furnish very little information regarding the growth and progress of Cranbrook. An occasional name is to be found ; Bettenham and Saxonhurst are two mentioned in a deed dated 1200, but for the rest it is only possible to conjecture the slow development that took place.

CHAPTER IV

THE SEVEN HUNDREDS

" Our common safety must be now the care."
—" The Illiad," Pope.

The origin of the Hundred goes far back to the early days of Anglo-Saxon history, in the years before the Conquest it furnished the framework upon which the judicial and financial systems were build. At a very early period the countryside was organised into groups of about ten householders who were mutually responsible for the good behaviour of each other. Generally known as a tithing, it was termed in Kent a borough, from the Old English word "borh," meaning a pledge or a surety. The Kentish office of borsholder is derived from the same source, meaning the " elder " or senior of the pledges. The Hundreds contained a number of these small groups, possibly the name may have indicated at some period a group of ten.

Furley expressed the view that many of the denes in the Weald had been formed into burhs or boroughs before, or at least very shortly after the Conquest, and that they were then consolidated into Hundreds. These Hundreds in the Weald, still difficult of access, would be benefited by a court, which, though subsidiary to the Shire Court at Penenden Heath, would bring justice home to the people. The King therefore established the Court of the Seven Hundreds, and appointed a Bailiff over them.

The origin is similar to that of the Chiltern Hundreds, with which most people are familiar in connection with the House of Commons. The original Hundreds were those of Barkley, Barnfield, Blackborne, Cranbrook, Rolvenden Selbritten and Tenterden. The last-named was withdrawn at a later date and added to the Cinque Ports. The fees of the Seven Hundreds were usually farmed out ; in the reign of Henry III for £5 a year, later £10 a year was paid by Stephen de Penshurst. They were granted to Sir John Norris of Hemsted in 1730, and thenceforth followed the Hemsted estate, Thomas Law Hodges paying £1,010 for the fee in 1817. The annual Court Leet of the Hundred of Cranbrook continued to be held at the George in Cranbrook until after the middle of the 19th century, but as with the manor courts, the dues were so trifling that the expense of the Court could no longer be justified and it ceased to function.

It is important to point out that the parish as we know it today had not developed at this early date ; for the purpose of administration and finance, as in Saxon days, the Hundred continued to be the civil authority.

The Hundred of Cranbrook extended over a greater area than the modern parish, including as it did much of Frittenden and a large part of the south side of Staplehurst, it was divided at first into four boroughs, Smithditch on the east comprising the Sissinghurst of today and extending as far as Three Chimneys, Bela Cregge, later Faircrouch, on the west including Glassenbury, North boro' and West boro'. These boroughs are first recorded towards the end of the reign of Henry III, later the number increased and some of the names were altered.

From the middle of the 13th century a rather more detailed picture emerges. By this time many of the denes originally held by one tenant had extended the area of cultivation and contained a number of householders. Some had expanded into villages and hamlets, including Cranbrook, where a stone church had been built before the year 1290 ; and at least one manor, that of Saxenhurst or Sissinghurst had come into being, taking its name from the dene originally part of the Manor of Westgate, Canterbury, and owned by the Archbishop.

The extracts from the earliest Plea Rolls, those of 1241, published by Furley in his History of the Weald, contain a number of items relating to the Hundred of Cranbrook.

" William, son of Alexander de Swetindene (Swattenden) was crushed to death by a certain beam. Judgment: misfortune."

" Richard the Salter was found killed in the house of William de Iden. It is unknown who killed him: murder."

" Amicia de Sussex, taken with stolen cloths, in Cranebroc comes and acknowledges (the fact) and the jury say she is guilty."

20

" John son of Simon at the Cross, and Cecily de Kadekerigge, were found killed in the house of the aforesaid Cecily by unknown malefactors in the borough of Smetheditch."

This last entry is of some interest for it mentions the dene of Karkeregge, an early name for Milkhouse Street, and is also one of the few references to the borough of Smithditch.

Crimes of violence were prevalent, and the responsibility for the maintenance of law and order, the apprehension of malefactors and bringing them to justice, rested on the inhabitants of each individual borough. Failure to detain criminals, or in the case of death by misadventure, delay or omission to report the case to the coroner resulted in a fine being imposed on all the householders collectively.

An incident reported a few years later in the early years of the reign of Edward I reveals another aspect of justice. Six men were drinking in a tavern in the borough of West (which included the central portion of the Hundred). A quarrel started and " one struck another on the head with a stick, so that he died." The guilty man pleaded clergy, and whilst the others were sent to gaol at Maidstone he was handed over to the Church authorities. Almost anyone who could barely read and write could claim the benefit of clergy and have his case remitted to the ecclesiastical courts, where punishment would be less severe.

By the close of the 13th century the whole area of the Weald had been settled, some improvement in the roads had taken place and in summer at least, travelling was not too difficult. Edward I constantly passed through the district and on two occasions he spent a night in Cranbrook. In June 1299, starting from the Manor House of the Abbot of Battle at Wye, he journeyed to the Archbishop's Manor at Charing, the next day he came to Cranbrook where he spent the night of June 19th, going on to New Romney the next morning and returning the following day to Lamberhurst.

Six years later, on his way to Chichester he passed through the Weald again, this time spending the night of July 1st, 1305 at Milkhus. (This is the earliest reference to Milkhouse that can be traced under that name). It was on this journey that the young Prince of Wales (afterwards Edward II, and the first bearer of that title) being out of favour with his father and forbidden the Court, determined to follow the King at a short distance until he obtained his pardon ; a letter written by him shows that on this date when the King stayed at Milkhouse, the Prince passed the night at Tenterden.

Another indication of the growing importance, and increasing population of Cranbrook may be observed in the grant of a market to the Rectory of Cranbrook by Edward I in 1289, at the request of Archbishop Peckham, and also two annual fairs to be held at St. Dunstan's day and in September at the feast of St. Giles. Fairs were religious rather than commercial in origin, being the occasions of the assemblies of the congregation on the feast days of Saints ; they could only be set up by a royal grant and usual custom granted this privilege to the church. In course of time they came to be a source of revenue of some importance. In the days when towns were less accessible the fair served a useful function in the economic life of the countryside, to which it brought some of the benefits of the town ; the itinerent traders and the local craftsmen offered a variety of necessary articles for sale ; earthenware, leather goods, salt, fish, sweetmeats, and cloth, were displayed side by side with implements for the farm, knives, and other useful or unusual merchandise. After the serious business of the fair came the merry-making and fun.

Both the market and the fairs of Cranbrook flourished through many centuries but the turnpike roads built during the 18th century resulted in the towns becoming more accessible and reduced the importance of these local gatherings, whilst the opening up of the railroads in the 19th century dealt the final blow to their usefulness.

Tradition enabled them to struggle on for a few years, but the fair became a mere occasion for uproar, the market had neither buyers nor sellers and so both institutions quietly ceased to be held.

CHAPTER V

THE COMING OF THE CLOTHIERS

" .... the woof unroll'd
Is by the noisy fulling-mill received."
—" The Fleece," Dyer.

There had been little in the history of Cranbrook up to
the year 1331 to distinguish it from many another small rural
community. Over the years the forest had been cleared and
brought into cultivation by hard work, but the Weald was
far away from the large towns, communications with them
were still difficult, especially in winter, and the course of
events in the greater world had few repercussions in this
remote district.

All this was changed by the decision of Edward III to
wrest from the Netherlands the monopoly they enjoyed of the
manufacture of high quality cloth. This decision entailed a
complete reversal of our traditional trade policy, for wool had
been for many years the greatest item in the export trade of
the country, more than 35,000 sacks being sent abroad in
the year 1310 (a sack of wool weighed 364 lb.).

The export duty of 40s. a sack furnished the Treasury
with the greatest part of its revenue. Much of this wool
was produced in the Cotswolds and many of the growers
had amassed large fortunes, but their interests suffered from
the monopoly established by the merchants of the Staple
who paid low prices to the grower and charged high prices to
the foreign buyer.

In furtherance of his policy of creating a prosperous
industry manufacturing a cloth that would compare favourably
with the products of the looms of Flanders, the King granted
passports to a number of clothmakers and their servants to
enable them to enter this country for the purpose of " working
wool and exercising their mystery." Flanders was then the
industrial centre of Western Europe, and Ghent, from whence
the newcomers came, had long held pride of place for the

excellence of the work of the weavers and clothmakers who plied their trade within the walls of the city.

It was in 1331 that these first Flemish craftsmen came to England, and there is a tradition that one of them named Kemp settled in Cranbrook, which had been selected as a suitable centre for the manufacture of the well-known broadcloth, but evidence is lacking and this same John Kemp is claimed to be the founder of the cloth industry at Kendal.

Clothmaking was no new craft in England, for it had been woven as far back as the Roman days, but much of this locally produced fabric was of poor quality, loosely woven, dense in texture and in need of shearing and shrinking. A better quality product, made in the towns, was expensive to buy, largely because of the restrictive practices and policies of the craft guilds.

In producing a superior quality of cloth, one of the most important technical advances of this period concerned the process of fulling. This had for long been done in Flanders by means of water power, and although fulling mills were in use in England from the early 13th century, the method usually employed was that of treading—the cloth being arranged in tubs in which a man stood, the length being moved at intervals to give every part an equal share of treading.

Another method laid the cloth on a long table where it was methodically pounded by hand.

The introduction of water power for the process turned the attention of the clothiers to those parts of the country where running water could be found, the many small streams around Cranbrook, running through narrow valleys easily dammed to regulate the flow offered ideal conditions. In addition, a plentiful supply of oak for the construction of the mills, with ample quantities of marl or fullers earth on the spot supplied further reasons for the choice of the site.

The location of several of these fulling mills is recorded in old deeds, but there is little that can be observed at the present day other than the remains of the bays of the ponds.

A fulling mill was a simpler machine than a grist mill, and required less construction of a durable nature.

When the cloth came from the weavers it had to be first scoured with wooden hammers in a trough of water. It was then stretched on racks to dry ; after drying it was rubbed over with the fullers earth, folded, and then placed beneath the heavy wooden hammer, which rose and fell as the water wheel slowly turned.

The dull sound of the hammer falling on the cloth, a deep " boom, boom " must have become very familiar to the people of Cranbrook after the cloth trade became well established.

This process of fulling played a most important part in the production of the broadcloth in which the clothmakers of the Weald excelled. It gave a firm and solid texture to the cloth and ensured a smooth surface, as well as cleaning the grease from the wool. After fulling, the cloth again went to be stretched out on the racks, and if this stretching was done too severely it could result in extra length being given to it ; evidently there were cloth makers who practised this form of dishonesty for an act passed in the reign of Edward VI laid down that " every piece of broadcloth that should be made in the Shire of Kent must contain in length, when thoroughly wet, between 28 and 30 yards, in breadth $1\frac{3}{4}$ yards at least, and when thicked, scoured, milled and fully dried, should weigh 84 lbs. at the least."

The racks on which the cloth was spread out were fitted with iron hooks to hold it in place, these racks were known as tenters and give us our present-day expression of " being on tenter-hooks." The fields in which these racks stood were the " tenter " field ; there are several fields in Cranbrook called the " tainter," but whether this name is derived from the tenter field is uncertain.

The industry quickly took root, and soon spread to the neighbouring villages in the Weald ; it is open to question whether the introduction of the Flemish craftsmen and the general policy of Edward III was entirely the reason for this rapid expansion of the clothing industry, not only in Cranbrook but in other rural areas of England.

It can be attributed in part to the attitude of the urban crafts and guilds, who by attempting to keep up the price of their products, and the restrictions imposed on their members, were hastening the decay of their industry in the towns.

With the transfer to the country districts there came into existence a new class of capitalist clothier. The manufacture of raw wool into good broadcloth called for many different crafts. The clothier bought the wool and distributed it for carding and spinning in the cottages. The spun wool was collected and passed to the weavers, shearers, fullers, and dyers in turn. All this called for capital far beyond the means of the individual weaver. The cloth had then to be despatched to the port of shipment if intended for export, or to London. The clothier thus combined the functions of capitalist, employer, and merchant, and most of the credit for the rapid growth of the broadcloth trade in Cranbrook is due to this new class that sprang up in the parish. Two of the earliest families to rise to wealth and prominence as clothiers here, appear to have no connection with the Flemish immigrants introduced by Edward III. The Henleys of Coursehorn were resident there in Edward I's reign, when according to Hasted, Gervase Henlie is mentioned in an Inquisition Post Mortem after the death of the last of the Handloe's of Buckhurst. The Sheafe family are recorded in Norwich in the early 14th century, and there are indications that the Courthopes and other of the local clothier families may be also traced back to an earlier period. However that may be, it is certain that by the close of the 15th century four or five of these merchants and capitalists had amassed considerable property in the parish and elsewhere and were able to exert an increasing influence in local affairs.

This period of prosperity for Cranbrook lasted for little more than two centuries, but during this comparatively short time, a pattern and form was given to the town which has endured to the present day.

In the meantime, during these early days of the new industry, much general discontent in Kent and elsewhere suddenly flared up into the rebellion of 1381, under the leadership of Wat Tyler and John Ball.

There must have been many men from Cranbrook among the supporters of the movement ; John de Beaghendenn (a name derived from that of a dene between Milkhouse and Golford) is named as one of a party that broke into the house of the parson of Appledore, his name is included in the list of the leaders of the revolt not granted the benefits of the general pardon. John Fynce, a carpenter from Cranbrook, took part in the destruction of the parsonage at Staplehurst, after which the mob moved on to Maidstone where they broke open the gaol before going on to London.

The rest of the story is part of our general history, but there appears to have been a sequel in the Weald after it became apparent that the promises given to the rebels by Richard II were being broken.

The following September, two Cranbrook men, Robert and John Crothole, were arrested with others for rebellion and treason at Linton and Maidstone, after having assembled near Milkhouse in order to force the King to " repeat and confirm all the liberties and charters granted at Mile End."

They were tried and convicted, being sentenced to death.

More than forty years after Wat Tyler's revolt the name of Beaghynden again appears, this time in connection with a curious case involving witchcraft.

About the early part of 1437, Cranbrook church was entered by thieves who stole some of the valuable ornaments and, what was worse, assaulted and killed the sexton who had attempted to prevent them getting away. The murderers escaped with their booty leaving no clue to their identity, to the distress and perplexity of the parishioners.

Two men whose names are given as Thomas Taillour and Robert Adcock, taking advantage of the general atmosphere of suspicion and distrust, conspired, under the pretence of tracing the authors of the crime by divination, to work off a personal grudge against certain of their neighbours, by prompting the " medium " to denounce them. Five persons were accused, three of them being brothers named Beggynden, all husbandmen or tenant farmers ; the séance having taken place at the Nag's Head in Southwark. Four of the accused were arrested and sent to Canterbury prison, the fifth one, Thomas Barlynge, became demented and unfit to plead.

The father of the three brothers thereupon petitioned the Chancellor that he would give orders for a full investigation into the charges preferred against his sons " by sorcery and witchcraft falsely and wickedly accused." The whole story is told at length by Aymer Vallance in Volume 43 of " Archæologia Cantiana," the ultimate fate of the prisoners is not known, although one of the brothers received a pardon without being brought to trial.

The whole business may have had more than local interest, for one of those taking part in the séance is stated to have been page to the Duke of Gloucester, whose wife was known to consult soothsayers and was currently believed to

have had recourse to magic and the black art. The story
shows that Cranbrook was no longer an isolated community
deep in the forest, instead we have indications of easy
communications with London and familiarity with the affairs
of the world at large.

CHAPTER VI

THE GOLDEN AGE

" Cloth of frize, be not too bold
Though thou art matched with cloth of gold."

The first half of the 15th century witnessed a period of disaster and distress following the death of Henry V.

The long-drawn-out war with France, resulting in the expulsion of the English from that country except for a foothold at Calais brought with it the loss of our market for cloth in Gascony. The quarrel with the Duke of Burgundy closed for a time the Flemish towns to our commerce, a further serious blow to the export trade. At home the Wars of the Roses dragged wearily on, and in Kent there occurred the rising under Jack Cade in protest against the financial oppression and incompetence of the government. Cade's effort to obtain redress was no mob movement, for his supporters included nearly 100 " Esquires and Gentlemen."

In several Hundreds the constables duly, and seemingly with legal authority, summoned out their men. The Abbot of Battle and the Prior of Lewes supported the rising.

Among the names of those who received a pardon for their part in the undertaking we find John Roberd of Cranbrook, and his son John, both of Glassenbury, the father being described as yeoman and the son as gentleman. There are only two other names from Cranbrook in a list which contains several thousands of names, although places such as Smarden and Pluckley sent their men in hundreds. This seems to suggest that in Cranbrook and the other cloth villages the people were less disposed to throw in their lot with the rebels than were the agricultural villages, possibly the growing prosperity of the industry accounts for this.

There is little doubt that despite the setbacks abroad and this unrest at home the production of broadcloth increased, the clothiers became more firmly established in

Cranbrook and the Weald and began to amass much property and wealth.

Already a start had been made in rebuilding the parish church of St. Dunstan, a work that was to continue for the next hundred years.

The second half of the century tells a different story. For fifty years the continent had enjoyed comparative peace, our markets were again opened there and the export of cloth developed at an enormous rate, to reach its peak in the early years of the 16th century.

For the clothiers of Cranbrook it was a time of prosperity never before experienced, and they were quick to take advantage of it, how successful they were may be gathered from information contained in some of the early wills. The Henley's of Coursehorn were one of the first of these families to attain prominence, Thomas Henley, who died in 1495, disposed of more than thirty properties in Cranbrook alone, with others in Biddenden, Tenterden, Romney and East Kent. His children and grandchildren intermarried with the land-owning families. Gervase Henley entered the Inns of Court, and his grandson Walter was knighted.

The Sheaffs were another example of the economic and social progress that the 16th century brought to the cloth-makers; Thomas Sheaff died in 1520—leaving to his sons much property that included Shepherds, Bakers Cross, Hancocks and the Freight.

Two other wealthy clothiers who died a few years later were John Curthop or Courthope, and William Lynch.

The basis for this successful development of the cloth trade in Cranbrook was the export market. Trade treaties negotiated in the reign of Edward IV had opened up the important districts of Flanders, still pre-eminent in the dyeing and finishing processes, production in Cranbrook tended to concentrate more and more on supplying these Flemish merchants with partly-finished cloths. This policy yielded handsome returns for many years, but it led to the neglect of other markets, in particular those of the Mediterranean, which passed into the hands of the West Country clothiers and the Bristol merchants. Coloured cloths were still made here, we read of a Cranbrook clothier supplying Christ Church, Canterbury with russett cloth in 1499, as late as 1610 the boys of Eton were being clothed in cloth described as

" sad Kent " and " sad blue " in colour, made in Cranbrook, but this supply to the home market formed a very small proportion of the total output of the looms of the Weald, which amounted to 12,000 pieces or lengths of cloth annually.

For nearly a century the industry enjoyed an almost unbroken period of great prosperity, but in 1566 an Act was passed to prohibit the export of unwrought or unfinished cloths ; designed to provide more employment at home, it brought disastrous consequences to the clothiers of the Weald. Already handicapped by the increase in the cost of production that followed the rehabilitation of the currency after the debasement in previous reigns, they suddenly found the chief outlet for their goods blocked. It was now that the results were brought home to them of the dangers of a policy of putting all the " eggs in one basket." Despite the general fall in trade in the latter half of Elizabeth I's reign, the other cloth districts gradually recovered their prosperity, but for Cranbrook and the Weald the blow had been mortal, and although the industry lingered on for another hundred years it never regained even a part of its former greatness.

But all this did not appear likely in 1573, when Queen Elizabeth I visited Cranbrook. A temporary improvement in business following the political unrest in the Netherlands seemed to foretell prosperous times ahead, and there were many tangible indications of the accumulated wealth acquired in recent times. The church had just been completed by the raising of the clerestory over the middle aisle and the extension of the east end, resulting in the beautiful building that is substantially unaltered to-day. New houses had been built, and the older ones renewed and enlarged ; Sissinghurst, where the Queen spent three days as the guest of Richard Baker, son of Sir John " Bloody " Baker, was a splendid example of the period, displaying much beautiful Tudor brick work together with the earlier form of timber and plaster. The George Inn, where the Queen alighted to receive the loyal address of welcome from the townsmen, had been almost entirely rebuilt only a few years earlier.

Coming from Bedgebury, after her stay in the town, Her Majesty proceeded to Coursehorn to inspect a cloth factory (the duties and customs expected of Royalty do not much change), where it is possible she saw work in progress in the cloth hall, today The Old Cloth Hall. It would be pleasant to think that the story of the road being covered with scarlet broadcloth for the Queen to walk upon from the town to Coursehorn had some authority to support it, but it seems likely that it is derived from the tradition of red carpet or cloth laid down at the door of the George when she alighted from her horse.

The bellringers were paid one shilling to ring a special peal " for the Queen's Majesty " (there were then five bells), and it must have appeared that the town had celebrated a great occasion. In the light of later developments it did in fact mark the most splendid moment in the history of the town.

The iron industry, which had always been an important factor in the economy of the Weald of Kent and Sussex, never figured very largely in the affairs of Cranbrook. There were, it is true, two furnaces situated at the extreme east and west ends of the parish. The Bedgebury furnace, partly in Cranbrook, partly in Goudhurst and recorded by the present Furnace and Forge farms, never had a very large output. John Browne the Horsemonden ironmaster states in 1637 that he only continues the use of " one ancient furnace in Cranbrook." By 1664 it had been discontinued, but in that year again " repaired and stock'd upon account of the warre."

Hammer Mill, at the other end of the parish, is actually in Biddenden, although it formed a part of the Sissinghurst estate and was charged with the maintenance of the bridge over the stream.

It was leased to Sir Richard Butler in the reign of Elizabeth I, but not long after appears to have been converted into a corn mill. It is probable that both these furnaces were chiefly employed in the production of iron in satisfaction of the considerable local industrial demand.

The ironworks in Cranbrook were never of any great importance compared to the cloth trade, but nevertheless the clothiers attributed the falling off in their trade in some measure to be connected with the general increase in the production of iron in the Weald, and went so far as to petition Parliament to pass a Bill to prohibit the erection of any new furnaces in the neighbourhood and to impose restrictions on those already existing.

This once prosperous cloth industry has left few indications of its importance that are discernible at the present day, and it is only by taking note of the large proportion of 16th and early 17th century houses in the town

Dr. Hugh Price (Ap. Rhys)
Vicar of Cranbrook, 1533-54

*St. Dunstan's Church from the North-West, showing the
Early 15th Century Tower*

Restored Tudor Fireplace from the Manor House of Coursehorne, the Seat of the Henley Family which was dug up in the garden

By courtesy of the Kent Archaeological Society

The second Market House, built in 1812; demolished 1860

The White Lion Inn and High Street, 1900

and outlying districts built by the clothiers to serve both as homes and business premises, that an appreciation of the predominant position held by the industry can be learned. These many fine houses and a church unusually large and beautiful for a country parish church are the real permanent memorials of the great period of the cloth making in Cranbrook.

CHAPTER VII

THE BEACONS

" Far on the deep the Spaniard saw, along each southern Shire,

Cape beyond cape, in endless range, those twinkling points of fire."

—Macaulay.

Queen Elizabeth I reigned for thirty years after her visit to Cranbrook in 1573, and for most of this time the gradual decline in the fortunes of the town was not readily apparent. A partial resumption of the export trade in unfinished cloths enabled the clothiers to hope that the better times of earlier days would again be experienced.

There was a growing uneasiness, especially in the counties of the south coast, of the intentions of Philip of Spain and the threat of invasion by the Spanish forces massed on the other side of the Channel. Earlier in the reign the French had caused the Queen's government some concern, and measures had then been approved which laid down the number of men who were to be mustered, their arms and equipment and places of assembly, providing also for a period of training every year. The certificate of the Musters of the Seven Hundreds taken in 1572 shows that their military strength amounted to 1,200 men, including 150 archers and 200 harquebuziers or men armed with a heavy hand gun, the forerunner of the musket ; there were 23 mounted men and the rest were classified as pikemen or billmen. Each Hundred mustered under its own officers, and two captains were appointed to command the whole detachment.

The plans to meet the threatened attack from Spain provided for a force of nearly 6,500 men, from that part of the county within reach of the sea, to muster for the defence of the coast.

Attention was given to the beacons or fire signals, by which the alarm could be raised quickly if a landing should be attempted.

The beacon at Cranbrook stood at Hartley, the site is recorded by the name of a field at Bull farm adjoining the road from Goudhurst. This beacon was first set up as far back as the last year of the reign of Edward II, in 1327. In the next reign a fixed plan provided for the setting up of six beacons in the Seven Hundreds. The warning signal would be received from Fairlight and passed on to four special beacons at Westwell, Coxheath, Ightham and Birling, and so on to the next chain of lights. Henry IV confirmed the arrangements and further ordered that the Seven Hundreds should be charged with the maintenance of eighteen men to serve these beacons. These orders remained unchanged over a long period, and were current at the time of the Spanish Armada in 1588.

Although the defeat of this attempt at invasion appeared so decisive, similar efforts were feared for some years after, and the upkeep of the watch at the beacons continued to be strictly maintained, and led to a long and angry dispute between the Seven Hundreds and Lydd. By the Act of Henry IV referred to above, it was laid down that in addition to the provision and maintenance of the beacons, a system of coast watchers, ready to give warning of an attempted landing by enemies of the realm, often pirates, should be organised by those Hundreds that adjoined the sea, or were within easy reach thereof. In 1585, when the Spanish Armada was first expected to attack our shores, the Lord Lieutenant of the County sent an order to the Seven Hundreds to provide 12 men for this sea guard at Dengemarsh, in view of the imminence of the threatened danger they agreed to comply with the order although never previously called upon for this service. In their own words, " wee did most willingly undertake as well in regarde to ye present danger then thought to be at hand as also to testify our obedience to our Lord Lieutenant thinking that change to have exceeded only by virtue of that his absolute authority, and not by pretence of any ordinary right or duty in lawe. But when we perseved that service was laide upon us by the earnest solistation of ye inhabitants of Lydd upon information that ye same was due by lawe, and feeling that ye burden of finding ye said 12 men to watch ye saide place, wole growinge to ye sume of ninescore pounds yearly at ye least, and considering ye saide watch if it shold have continuance wold charge us and our posterities for ever, Mr. Thomas Roberts, esquier, in the yere 1587, sent Stephen Sharpy and Edwarde Batcocke with a petition enclosed in his letter unto our Lord Lieutenant that we might have a daye apoynted that ye men of Lydde might show by what right they challenged this service at our hands."

A meeting took place at Ashford in accordance with this request at which Sir Thomas Scot, a deputy lieutenant presided, and although "the matter was thoroughly handled on our side by Mr. Roberts with our councell" Sir Thomas Scot would not give a decision until their councell and others had met in London and set down their opinions in writing.

Not satisfied with this result, Mr. Roberts sent Sharpy and Batcocke post haste to Dover where Lord Cobham, the Lord Lieutenant, was about to embark for the Netherlands on a mission. He referred the two petitioners to William Lambarde who "tooke a breefe out of our booke and certified our L.L. of ye wronge we had, whereupon ye Lord Lieutenant called Ste Sharpy and Ed Batcocke unto him requesting them that they wold have patience and maintaine ye watch until he returned again out of ye Lowe Countries." Before his return the Armada had been defeated and the Lord Lieutenant discharged the watch, at the same time appointing William Lambarde and Humphrey Winham to look into the dispute between the Seven Hundreds and Lydd, who gave as their opinion that the matter should be tried before a jury at common lawe. This view was rejected by Lydd and in 1589 "by reason of sume sturres upon ye narrow seas watches were commanded to be kept and Sir Thomas Scot sent straight commandment unto Sir Richard Baker and Mr. Roberts that ye Seven Hundreds shold watch at Dengemarshe with 12 men, and Sir Richard Baker made his warrants unto ye constables and wold have had Mr. Roberts set his hand to the said warrant but Mr. Roberts refused." Sir Thomas Scot then went to Lord Cobham, but the Lord Lieutenant told him that the previous service by the Seven Hundreds had been at his order, and that he saw no reason now to command them to undertake this duty. The next step was a request by Sir Thomas Scot for a meeting with the two parties at Ashford, this did not please the Cranbrook men who refused to go, whereupon the whole matter was laid before the Lords of the Council in the form of a complaint that the watch at Dengemarsh had not been maintained. The question at issue thus passed out of the hands of the Lord Lieutenant; the next move was to find someone who would present the case for the Seven Hundreds before the Council, and Mr. Roberts requested " Mr. Dr. Giles Fletcher to deale for ye Seven Hundreds that was of credit amongst ye Lords of ye Councell and to follow their cause before them . . ."

Giles Fletcher was the son of Richard Fletcher, Vicar of Cranbrook until his death in 1586 ; he filled several important offices of state and later became Ambassador to Russia. He had married, in 1580, Joan Sheafe, daughter of Thomas Sheafe, a leading clothier ; their two sons, Phineas and Giles, were poets of no mean standard. With these local connections it is evident that his selection to present the case for the Hundreds was a wise choice, and in fact he obtained an order for the dismissal of the case as the men of Lydd excused themselves from appearing before the Council saying " their warninge was too short," but Lord Cobham intervened to suggest that nevertheless they should be given an opportunity to present their case. Finally, after dragging on for two years, the whole business was remitted to Quarter Sessions at Canterbury, where " seven bills of inditment under ye statute of watches 3. Henry 4 were then put in to ye Grand Jureye by ye men of Lydd," but the Grand Jury refused to find a true bill, and there the controversy ended.

William Lambarde, whose name appears twice in the account of the proceedings, was the eminent lawyer and antiquary, Justice of the Peace for Kent and author of " Perambulation of Kent," published in 1576.

Sir Richard Baker had been knighted by Queen Elizabeth in 1573 ; Thomas Roberts, who fought so stubbornly for the rights of the Seven Hundreds, was son of Walter Roberts of Glassenbury ; knighted in 1603, he was afterwards created the first baronet.

The beacon at Cranbrook continued in use for many more years, although only manned in times of danger.

Lambarde states that before the time of Edward III the beacons were made of great stacks of wood, but that about the eleventh year of his reign it was ordained that in Kent they should be high standards with their pitchpots.

The Tenterden beacon of this type was fixed to the tower of the church, but at Cranbrook it consisted of a high tripod structure standing in an open field.

It was Lord Cobham who caused all the beacons in Kent to be plotted or mapped, with direction lines between them in order, as Lambarde says, " by which any man, with little labour, may be assured where the danger is, and thereof inform his neighbours."

CHAPTER VIII

THE PURITANS

" And blame me not for disrespect
If I the flatt'rers style reject."

—John Gay.

When Elizabeth came to the throne in 1558, she was at once faced by a grave potential danger in the conflict over religion.

The Elizabethan Church was designed to appeal to as wide a range of people as possible, it essayed to satisfy everybody and succeeded only in obtaining at first a grudging acceptance from the majority who were heartily weary of the changes, persecutions and unrest that they had undergone during the preceeding ten or more years.

Within a few years some of these lukewarm friends were to become outspoken critics and even enemies of the Establishment.

The origin of the Puritan movement must be sought on the Continent and in the teaching of John Calvin. Many English supporters of the Reformation had sought safety in exile in the Rhineland, the Low Countries and Geneva when Mary ascended the throne, in order to maintain their faith from a Catholic Queen.

Under foreign influences and associations, some renounced the Book of Common Prayer of Edward VI which they had taken with them in their exile ; all returned with a burning zeal for the salvation of their country.

The Puritans were assured that they were numbered among the " elect," they held a depth of conviction and could rise to a height of exaltation beyond the comprehension of those who did not share their beliefs.

The early Elizabethan Church numbered many sympathisers of Calvinistic teaching among the clergy, who were anxious for the Presbyterian system, already established in Scotland, to be set up in England. To them the Church should stand for truth and the rule of the Scriptures ; the Established Church appeared to set uniformity before truth and conformity before conscience.

The Puritans laid great stress on their preaching and their own high standard in this matter was noteworthy ; another method of expounding their views took the form of fortnightly meetings of local clergy for discussion groups, to which the laity were admitted.

The conflict for the control of the Church took a new phase with the publication of two tracts by Thomas Cartwright, who held a Chair of Divinity at Cambridge until he was dismissed in 1570.

All these happenings did not pass unnoticed in Cranbrook, where from the beginning of the century a strongly sympathetic bond had been forged between the clothiers and their customers in Antwerp and the Netherlands. While the majority of the parishioners shared the lukewarm views common to most of the country, yet there existed a minority who favoured the new current of Calvinism running through the Church. These views were reinforced when John Stroud, sometime Vicar of Yalding, came to Cranbrook to help the Rev. Richard Fletcher, the Vicar.

Stroud had already been in trouble with the Chancellor of the Diocese of Rochester for printing and disposing of certain books containing seditious matter, and had been ordered to leave the diocese within forty days. He appealed to the Archbishop, who reversed the order and granted a preaching licence enabling him to return to his parish of Yalding. But he soon found himself before the Rochester authorities, this time for being too active in disseminating the works and writings of Thomas Cartwright, and was again forced to leave his parish, coming shortly afterwards to Cranbrook. Here he met with opposition to his views from some members of the congregation ; the Vicar persuaded his son Richard Fletcher—then Vicar of Rye and afterwards Bishop of London (perhaps better known as the father of John Fletcher, the collaborator with Beaumont)— to come to Cranbrook and preach in support of Mr. Stroud, who had been called in derision " A Printing Preacher." This did not quiet the stir and again the business was referred to the

Archbishop. Parker, whose sympathies were believed to lie with those eager for reform, had died in 1575 ; his successor, Dr. Grindall, suspended Stroud from preaching in order that he might examine the matter more fully.

Immediately petitions to the Archbishop in favour of Stroud poured in from most of the neighbouring parishes, signed by the ministers and churchwardens ; these were followed by another petition submitted by many of the important landowners of West Kent, and as a result the Archbishop lifted his ban and restored to John Stroud his license to preach.

A powerful speaker, he commenced the practise of preaching a sermon on Saturday—then the market day for Cranbrook—and his views must have exerted a considerable influence in the parish. He died in 1582 of the plague.

John Stroud was followed in Cranbrook by Dudley Fenner, a friend of Cartwright with whom he had worked at Antwerp, and an extreme puritan as witness the name of two of his sons who were baptized during his stay at Cranbrook : " More Fruit " and " Faint Not."

In the meantime the struggle within the Church grew more intense and the Queen decided that the time had come to take a more decided course ; Grindall died in 1583, and the new Archbishop to be appointed, John Whitgift, the most ardent anti Puritan of the bishops, had already championed the Church against Cartwright.

The leaders of the Presbyterian movement, including Cartwright, found themselves in prison ; a few fanatics who were prepared to imperil the state suffered death; all ministers were required to subscribe to three Articles of Conformity.

Dudley Fenner is numbered among those ministers who were unable and unwilling to subscribe to these articles, consequently he suffered suspension, and a few years later went to Holland where he died in 1589.

The Established Church had won its fight, but Puritanism could not be destroyed by persecution and the eventual division of the Protestant Church into Anglican and Nonconformist is witness to the clash of ideas so tragically opposed in the England of Elizabeth I.

For a time Cranbrook enjoyed a period of relative quiet. especially during the time that William Eddy was Vicar, but there was always a strong undercurrent of feeling sympathetic to the more extreme views that were being expressed in many parts of the country, church attendance, as required by law was observed generally, and the few obscure sects such as the Brownists, as the followers of Robert Brown came to be called, found little support except among the very poor.

During the reign of James I the exportation of unfinished cloths was again forbidden, this resulted in numbers of the workers leaving the Weald, where they could no longer find employment; most went to the Palatinate where they could follow their trade.

When Archbishop Laud was appointed to Canterbury he at once started to introduce many changes, prompted by the conviction that it was necessary to combat the rise of Puritanism, often founded on the personal eloquence of individual preachers without any set order or form of worship, by the reintroduction of much of the ritual and ceremony abolished in the early days of the Elizabethan Church; the Communion Table was again to be placed at the East End of the church, guarded by rails.

The Civil War had few repercussions in Cranbrook where the majority of the people were in sympathy with the Parliamentary cause, the local leaders Thomas Plummer, John Rabson and others were moderate in their views, as was the case with John Williamson the presbyterian minister appointed to succeed the Vicar.

There had been a protest from Cranbrook against the levy of Ship Money by Charles I, not on the grounds of the legality or otherwise of the tax, but because the parish had been assessed on the basis of a municipal borough. The appeal did not result in any tangible benefit, although a promise to make future assessments on the lower appropriate level may have given some satisfaction.

The few supporters of King Charles in the parish were carefully watched. Sir Walter Roberts and his son Walter were arrested when staying at the King's Head, Cranbrook in May 1648 on their way to London, by Major Gibbon and a party of horse. On giving an undertaking not to bear arms against the Parliament they were released and Major Gibbon " engaged that they should no more be troubled by his party nor have any more horses taken from them than those then took which were worth £60."

In 1659 the Council of State instructed the Militia Commissioners of Kent to remove to a safe place a considerable quantity of arms belonging to the State lying at Cranbrook and not properly secured against surprise.

After the Restoration the landowning and upper classes tended to support the Anglican Church, but among the tradespeople and middle classes, strong opinions in favour of Presbyterian and other non-conforming sects continued to be expressed. The struggle for recognition of the freedom of worship went on in the parish until the Toleration Act of 1689 freed the chapels and meeting houses from the restraints and restrictions under which they had laboured for so many years.

CHAPTER IX

THE GOOD EARTH

" But with my little I have much content.
Content hath all ; and who hath all is rich."

—Phineas Fletcher.

During the sixteenth and seventeenth centuries many changes took place in the ownership both of land and of manorial rights in Cranbrook.

The first reference to the Manor of Glassenbury is contained in a rental of Walter Roberts dated 1482.

Walter Roberts, son of John Roberts, who had been a supporter of Jack Cade, suddenly emerges into prominence. To quote the inscription on the Roberts Memorial in the church, " he built the Moated House in the Valley of Glassenbury, he was disseized of his Estate and forced to fly into sanctuary for endeavouring to conceal his friend and neighbour, Sir John Guildeforde, from the resentment of that cruel Prince King Richard ye 3rd, but was restored on the accession of King Henry ye 7th, became Sheriff of Kent in the fifth year of that reign, died in or about the year 1522 . . . . this gentleman had three wives, viz.: Margaret, Isabel, Alice."

He married as his second wife Isabel Culpeper of Bedgbury ; the Dene of Glassenbury was held of the Manor of Bedgbury, a rental dated 1464 for the Dene of Cranbrook, which extended over almost all the town, reveals that it was then held by Richard Culpepyr, a note written at the foot states, " I pay to the Prior of Christchurch for the hole rent 7s. yearly, and for sewte I pay . . . ."

It seems that Walter Roberts obtained a good deal of property as a result of his marriage, he also obtained permission to fence in and make a park of his lands in Cranbrook, Goudhurst and elsewhere, at the same time he resolved to constitute his property into a manor.

Glassenbury was not an original manor but consisted of a number of denes owned by many different manors for which a quit rent was paid, these quit rents amounted to much less than the quit rents he in turn exacted from his tenants.

Sissinghurst, on the contrary, had been a manor from the 13th century, part of the manor was bought by Richard Baker from the Barham family, who succeeded the Saxonhursts. Sir John Baker, son of Richard, purchased the rest of the manor and added to it other land he obtained as a result of the disposal of the possessions of the Religious Foundations ; in this way Flishinghurst and Hazelden denes came to be a part of Sissinghurst manor together with other property.

The dene of Angley, part of the Royal Manor of Wye, had always been the personal property of the Abbot of Battle, when the Abbey lands were disposed of Angley did not form a part of the general estate, being sold separately to Sir Walter Henley.

Little Chart manor passed into the hands of the Darrells, and the Bayham Abbey lands in Cranbrook became attached to the Glassenbury manor.

As a result of all these changes the long established links of Cranbrook with the monastic houses ceased to exist after these former church estates passed into lay ownership.

Many of the clothiers' houses were bought by new owners, following the decline in the cloth trade with the resultant departure of the families formerly engaged in this trade. As early as 1614 the Privy Council had instructed three local Justices of the Peace to enquire into and make the best agreement they can regarding a petition received from Richard Courthope of Cranbrook, clothier much impaired in his estate by " giving credit of his wares to certain heretofore of good estate but now decayed bankrupts." Courthope " is fallen into very great decay and is heavily in debt."

With this general decline in industry, attention turned again to agriculture, the cloth houses became farmhouses or tenements for the agricultural workers. The possibilities of hops and fruit had not yet been revealed, wheat and rye were grown in quantity for the two varieties of bread, rye bread being generally consumed by the poorer classes. Barley also, for the making of beer, oats in lesser degree for the horses and cattle were the other cereal crops. Meat consumption was on a very large scale, the raising of cattle and pigs for the local markets formed an important part of the economy of the farms. The soil yielded good crops, and the pasture, extensively dressed with marl, furnished first-class grazing.

The centre of the town was paved about the year 1657, at this time a market house stood in the middle of the road opposite the entrance to the church. A square building, it contained an upper storey for the storage of any grain not sold on the market day. The octagonal market house depicted in Dearn's "Weald of Kent" replaced the original building in 1814, being removed about fifty years later after the Vestry Hall had been built.

In the 17th century there were very few farms of any considerable size, most of the holdings consisting of a few acres worked by the husbandman and his family, sometimes as tenants, often as owners.

The yeoman farmer, possibly a clothier as well, farmed on a larger scale, and there were the estates of Sissinghurst and Glassenbury. As a centre for the surrounding countryside in days when travel presented much difficulty, Cranbrook filled an important place in the economy of the Weald, its craftsmen and tradesmen were able to supply most of the needs of the agricultural villages round about, thus helping to maintain a population more numerous than the reduced industrial activity of the town could otherwise have sustained.

Flax grew fairly extensively and although much of the crop supplied the domestic needs of the farmers, a certain amount went to the small local linen industry. The description "linen weaver" occurs in the registers during the 17th and 18th centuries.

The open-field system of cultivation found in many parts of England had never existed in Cranbrook and the Weald where all the open land had been won gradually from the forest, resulting in many small fields often less than an acre in size.

Rotation of crops was not practised and neither potatoes nor turnips had been introduced in the 17th century.

Although the well-known rhyme tells us that

"Turkeys, Heresy, Hops and Beer
Came into England all in one year"

hops were not grown in the Weald on any considerable scale before the early 18th century, since when they have played an ever-increasing part in the agricultural economy of Cranbrook and district.

The local market in hops during the 18th century was of some importance until the trade passed into the hands of the London factors.

In these early days the crop depended in the main on the weather, the season being a good one and favourable to the hops meant a satisfactory return for the grower, in the absence of any method of spraying or dusting to protect the plants from aphis and other pests it sometimes happened that no crop was picked; hops, however, were but one item among the crops raised on the average general farm of the period, the cost of growing them then bearing no comparison with the expenses of modern times, the failure of one particular crop did not unduly hurt the farmer.

Ash poles were more commonly used for poling the hops and farm account books for the 18th century often note as many items for the purchase of young ash plants as they do for the setts. Incidentally the farmers were able to sell their old hop poles as cord wood.

Coal for drying came by sea from South Wales, being then transported by barge to Newenden or Maytham wharf on the Rother. The charcoal, in the case of the larger farms, was burnt on the farm, the burner going on a regular round to do the " coling."

Prices of agricultural produce, in particular wheat, fluctuated greatly from year to year according to the harvest ; an early 18th century account book enables some idea to be formed of the cost of certain staple products :—

Butter sold at 4½d. a pound in 1725, wheat varied from 2s. 6d. to 8s. 6d. a bushel in one decade, a side of pork weighing 55 lb. cost 15s. 1d. and apples were 6d. and 1s. a bushel.

The small farmer of the period consumed most of the produce of his land, he had few needs that he could not satisfy as a result of his own efforts ; cheese seems to have been an exception to this general rule, for it is one of those articles usually included in a list of " shops goods " : sugar, salt, and other items not grown at home, that were bought from the shops in the town. Dutch cheese came from Holland by water, other varieties to be obtained were usually

Cheshire and Gloucester, the price of which was 3½d. a pound.

Fruit growing in the Weald is comparatively a modern development, the soil at one time being considered quite unsuitable for cherries, these were grown in East Kent for the London market on an extensive scale at least as early as the 17th century.

A few apples were planted in gardens and small orchards, but the idea of growing fruit on a commercial scale only really developed late in the 19th century, many of the specialised hop and fruit farms in Cranbrook were general mixed farms growing large crops of grain and hay less than one hundred years ago.

The fertile land on which we live is no longer the vital factor in our lives that our forbears knew it to be ; the mills that once ground the local wheat for the daily bread have ceased to revolve, the tractor needs imported oil instead of the oats and hay that fed the team of horses or oxen ; these and many other matters combine to weaken our appreciation of the dependence on Nature that earlier generations understood so well.

CHAPTER X

THE EXILES

" And took a long farewell, and wish'd in vain
For seats like these beyond the western main."

—" The Deserted Village," Oliver Goldsmith.

Men and women have gone out from every parish in the land to make new homes in many countries overseas. The early emigrants of the 17th century were seeking for a place where they could find freedom for the expression of their religious beliefs denied to them in their own country. In later years the motive that impelled them to go was mainly economic, for life in the rural areas in the early 19th century had become hard and comfortless, offering few opportunities of betterment.

In most cases they were soon forgotten in their native parish, but sometimes it is possible to follow their fortunes in the new country of their choice.

William Eddy, Vicar of Cranbrook, 1591-1616, married Mary Fosten of Cranbrook and they had a family of ten children, two dying in infancy. Their mother died in 1611 and the Vicar married a second time, to a widow with five children of her own. Soon afterwards, possibly following the death of their father in 1616 the Eddy children left Cranbrook and are next reported in Suffolk.

The brothers John and Samuel Eddy decided to cast in their lot with the early settlers in America and left England in the " Handmaid," landing at Plymouth, Mass., on October 29th, 1630. John was accompanied by his wife and two daughters. Shortly after, their two sisters, Abigail and Anne, sailed to join them on the " Lyon," reaching Boston in 1632.

John Eddy, a freeman of Watertown, was appointed the first Town Clerk of that settlement in 1635, a member of the first Governing Board, a member of the Militia and the first Church. He died in 1684, aged 87. Samuel remained at

Plymouth, being made a freeman of that town and died in 1687, aged 83. They had been joined by a nephew John, son of their brother, Zacharias, who stayed in England; the family multiplied and prospered, a large party of their descendants met to celebrate the " Tercentenary of the Eddy family in America," in 1930. One sister, Mary, remained in Cranbrook, having married Simeon Evenden.

Soon after this another company of about 25 families sailed for the New World, many of them coming from Cranbrook. This party was led by the Rev. Henry Whitfield of Ockley, Surrey. He had married Dorothy Sheafe, daughter of Dr. Thomas Sheafe, Dean of Windsor, and grand-daughter of Thomas Sheafe, our Cranbrook clothier. William Chittenden, another member of the party, was married to another grand-daughter, Joanna ; she afterwards married Abraham Cruttenden, also of the company.

Yet a third grand-daughter of Thomas, Margaret, daughter of Richard Sheafe of Shepherds and his wife, Margery Roberts, was married to Robert Kitchell of Rolvenden as his second wife; Robert's mother, Joan (Jordan) had married as her third husband Dr. Edmund Sheafe, he died in 1625 and Joan Sheafe therefore travelled with her son, her eldest daughter Joanna, mentioned above, by her marriage with Dr. Edmund Sheafe, as well as two other children of this marriage, Jacob and Mary.

The company sailed from England in the " St. John," of 350 tons, their first recorded act as a separate community was the Covenant which they signed on board the ship.

" We whose names are hereunder written, intending by God's gracious permission to plant ourselves in New England: We do faithfully promise each to each for ourselves and our families, and those that belong to us, that we will, the Lord assisting us, sit down and join ourselves together in one entire plantation, and to be helpful each to the other in every common work, according to every man's ability and as need shall require ; and we promise not to desert or leave the plantation but with the consent of the rest, or the greater part of the company who have entered into this engagement.

" As for our gathering together in a church way, and the choice of our officers and members to be joined together in that way, we do refer ourselves until such time as it shall please God to settle us in our plantation. In witness whereof we subscribe our hands the first day of June, 1639."

After a quiet passage of about seven weeks they landed at New Haven, Conn. in July 1639, settling in Guildford, Conn., a few months later.

From the sailing of the Mayflower (of only 180 tons) in 1620, it had been the religious motive that inspired these early settlers ; only one religion was tolerated in England and it was not the Puritan under the early Stuarts.

Some of these refugees wished to set up a state on the Geneva system where the teachings of Calvin would be forced on all who desired to settle there, but the groups who went to Connecticut, while wishing to enjoy religious freedom themselves were ready to extend it to others.

Not all the early settlers went for religious motives however, the Virginia Company and the Massachusetts Bay Company were financing emigration on a considerable scale and many were attracted by the opportunity to " better themselves." Thus, in 1635, the Minister of Cranbrook issued a certificate recommending Edward White, aged 42, husband-man of Cranbrook, Martha his wife and two children, Martha and Mary, who were sailing in the " Abigail " for New England.

The perils and discomforts of an Atlantic crossing in the small ships of two or three hundred tons were such as to daunt the spirit of all but the most determined hearts.

We get another glimpse of family migration in the Bigge family. John Bigge, an important clothier, left two sons and three daughters. John the son, a jurist of Maidstone, had only one son, who died before his father. Smallhope—born in 1584 (the name is an indication of the early rise of Puritanism in Cranbrook)—built the house at Wilsley Pound called Gaythorne, now known as the Pound House. On his death in 1638 without children, this property went to John and when he died it passed to the children of their sisters, one of whom had married John Stow of Rockbury in New England, and the other Hopestill Foster of Biddenden and Dorchester, New England.

They sold the property to William Boys, the conveyances were executed in America before the public notary for Massachusetts Colony in 1664, and are now deposited in the Archives of the Kent County Council at Maidstone, they are witnessed by a number of people including Jacob Sheafe, possibly the Jacob who went out with the Whitfield party in 1639. It is good to think that many of these names of former Cranbrook residents are frequently to be met with in North America at the present time.

In the late eighteenth century emigration was largely encouraged by many of the parish authorities—the growing population put a burden on the poor rates, the financial assistance given to families prepared to leave their native land to make a new start overseas seemed to be money well spent if it eased the claims for parish assistance. In Cranbrook the amount so spent often exceeded £100 a year; at the time that the Parish Farm at Sissinghurst Castle was giving good results these grants were made from the profits of that enterprise.

Many, of course, continued to leave on their own initiative encouraged by the reports of the wealth of the American continent and the prospects of a far better life than could be had at home, often to find that the reality was far less encouraging when they arrived on the other side of the Atlantic.

But the tide continued to flow outward, the 1830's and 1840's were bad times in England where there was great hardship and distress among the poor. Robert Pethurst, postmaster of Cranbrook notes in his diary of May, 1844: "My daughter Phebe, her husband Richard Odiam, and two sons and two daughters left Cranbrook for America, by rail to Liverpool." Thomas Pile notes in his diary for September, 1868: "Jonathan Oyler and three of his brothers from Goddards Green leave England to reside at River La Plate." Earlier in 1864 he noted: "Mr. George Shoobridge came home to Staplehurst last Sunday week and called to-day. On leaving he took with him a red rose bush to carry home to Harrison, Hamilton County, Ohio."

About this time another man, William Booth, left Cranbrook to try his fortune in America. His affairs prospered and his son, Mr. George G. Booth, created a rural estate about nineteen miles north of Detroit to which he gave the name of Cranbrook, derived from the birthplace of his father. The estate totals 260 acres of which 40 form the homestead property, the rest being held by various Trusts created by Mr. and Mrs. Booth, the most important of which is the Cranbrook Foundation for the establishment of an Academy of Arts. Other provisions provide for a School for Girls, and Cranbrook School for Boys ; a wide stretch of woodland is appropriately named Angley Wood.

In Australia, Cranbrook School, Sydney, a leading public school, maintains friendly contact with its more venerable namesake at home. Cranbrook has another link with Sydney, N.S.W.; in 1839 Robert Tooth started to send beer from the Bakers Cross brewery to Australia, the barrels went to Maidstone where they were loaded on barges and taken by water to the ships lying in the Thames. Shortly afterwards his son, Edward Tooth, went to Sydney and founded the brewery there, which has since expanded into the largest firm of brewers in Australia with a capital (1947) of six million pounds. Edward's wife died at Sydney leaving five children and he returned to England, later buying Little Stream farm ; he did not live long after this purchase, dying at Burton on Trent in 1858, being buried in Cranbrook churchyard.

Several families from Cranbrook emigrated to Western Australia in 1840.

The youngest settlement to bear the name of Cranbrook is the city of that name in British Columbia. A happy combination of prairie and mountain against the background of the Selkirk and Rocky Mountains, Cranbrook is conceded to be one of the prettiest as well as prosperous towns in British Columbia. Founded in 1903 by James Baker, who claimed kinship with the Bakers of Sissinghurst, the township grew apace and was granted the status of a city in 1953. Appropriately the main street is named Baker Street.

CHAPTER XI

THE QUIET YEARS

*" For these ancient places do not change, they
permit themselves to stand apart and to repose—by
paying that price—almost alone of all things in
England they preserve some historic continuity."*

—Belloc.

The years that followed the Restoration of the
Monarchy in 1660 were a period of quiet uneventful days
in Cranbrook—the change from the narrow discipline
enforced during the Commonwealth being welcomed at first
with general relief.

In London, Samuel Pepys at the Navy Office laboured
to restore order and efficiency to the Royal Navy, laying the
foundations upon which its future supremacy was built up.
In furtherance of his plans the House of Commons voted the
sum of more than half a million pounds " for the speedy
building of thirty ships of war, the sum to be raised, levied
and paid within the space of seventeen months commencing
March 25th, 1677."

Every taxation unit received a demand for the
proportion of this total sum thus authoriesd. Towards this
amount the Cranbrook assessment totalled £98, apportioned
between the six boroughs into which the original four
boroughs had been divided.

Faircrouch (£18 9s. 6d.), and North Boro' (£24 9s. 0½d.),
are two of the original names, but Smithditch and West Boro'
have disappeared, being replaced by Town Boro' (£14 3s. 2d.),
Crotholl (£20 8s. 1½d.), Kings Abbott (Angley, Friezley and
The Common) (£10 5s. 5½d.) and Outbonds (probably that
part of the former Boro' of Smithditch that extended into
Biddenden (£10 4s. 8½d.)

These six boroughs continued to be the areas of assessment for the Land Tax.

With the eighteenth century there followed a long period of little change for Cranbrook, where the events of the greater world outside found but few echoes. Certainly during Marlborough's campaigns a few officer prisoners of war were billetted in the town and at Goudhurst—the painted panels on a wall and door at Old Wilsley have been attributed to them —but their presence would have little effect on the even tenor of the life of a parish that had become mainly an agricultural community.

The weekly market on Saturday, the two annual fairs in May and September were important events in the calendar.

Among the leading families who for long years had led the parish—perhaps it could be called the period of the three baronets—important changes took place. The Henleys of Coursehorne moved from Cranbrook to their estate at Otham near Maidstone, and although they continued to own much property in the parish they ceased to take any part in local affairs.

At Sissinghurst the last baronet, Sir John Baker, died in 1661 at an early age, leaving three daughters as his co-heirs. His widow continued to reside at Sissinghurst until her death, the daughters had married and gone away from the parish and when the property was eventually divided amongst them the residence ceased to be occupied and stood empty for a long time.

For over two hundred years the Bakers had lived at Sissinghurst—their connection with the parish goes back even further—and had always taken a prominent part in the business of the parish, and the passing away of this family severed another link with the distant past.

Later in time a similar failure of heirs in the direct male line resulted in the Glassenbury estates passing to Jane Roberts, the only daughter, who married the Duke of St. Albans. The marriage turned out an unhappy event and the couple separated, the Duchess to live at Hunton. The Duke did not reside at Glassenbury and thus Cranbrook suffered the loss of the services of the third of its important families. Happily, on the death of the Duke of St. Albans the estate reverted to the younger Irish branch of the family and in due time the name of Roberts reappears to play once more a leading part in the public business of the parish.

A few of the old clothier families continued to live in Cranbrook although they no longer carried on the industry. Thus there were Hovendens at Friezley for a time, Westons at Wilsley, and Holdens. Another long established family of note, Plumer of Milkhouse Place, together with more recent newcomers, the Cookes of Swifts, gradually assumed the lead in many directions.

The population of Cranbrook decreased during all this century, when the first census was taken in 1801 it had fallen to 2,561, against an estimated figure of 3,500 to 4,000 in late Tudor years when an archdiaconal visitation in 1569 stated the number of householders to be 384 with 1,908 communicants, this at a period when the numbers were still increasing. The decline started early in the 17th century, the lowest figure being reached probably about 1770.

The improved state of the roads consequent on the passing of the early Turnpike Acts made travelling much easier between the villages of the Weald and the towns, this contributed in no small degree to the revival of Cranbrook as a market town and a shopping centre. The first road to be constructed, in 1763, connected Maidstone with Cranbrook and on to Tubs Lake. By 1770 this had been followed by others: Kippings Cross, Brenchley, Horsmonden, Goudhurst to Wilsley Green; Haselden Wood, Cranbrook to Appledore; Milkhouse Street to Biddenden; and Golford Green to Biddenden.

There were toll gates or turnpikes approximately every five miles, the turnpike trusts were authorized to collect the tolls from roads which they undertook to build and maintain. Writing in 1814, Dearn says the road from Maidstone to Cranbrook " with the exception of two miles between Staplehurst and Cranbrook is really a very good road, that it is passable by carriages is proved by the circumstances of a stage coach passing to and fro three times a week for some years past without a single accident that could be imputed to the road."

It was usual when repairing the roads to shoot down the stones where they were intended to lie just as they came from the quarry. In order that these stones should be broken up and worked into the carriage way, wagons with wheels 16 inches wide at one time paid no toll, afterwards they paid half the rate charged to vehicles with wheels of 6 inches. The early turnpikes were unpopular at first with the country people, who resented being called upon to pay a toll for using the King's Highway which, they contended, should be free and open to all.

With the better roads came improved travelling, the old stage coach with an average speed of not more than four miles an hour was overtaken by the fast mail coach carrying the Royal Mail at 8 or 10 miles an hour that superseded the Post Boys on horseback.

Travelling was not without its dangers, as the following advertisement from *The Times* of October 3, 1798 makes clear: " £200 Reward. General Post Office, July 3, 1798. The Post Boy carrying the Mail from Bromley to Sevenoaks last night was stopped between 10 and 11 o'clock by a single Highwayman who presented a Horse pistol and demanded the Mail, which the boy gave him. The Bags taken are those for Sevenoaks, Tonbridge, Lamberhurst, Battle, Rye and Hastings."

The completion of the turnpikes resulted in a network of tollgates around Cranbrook: at Knoxbridge, Three Chimneys, Golford Green, on the old Benenden road near Golford, Whitewell, and Hartley, with two inner ones on Windmill Hill and at Turnden.

It soon became almost impossible to journey anywhere without paying tolls every few miles, thus travel became expensive, although it did result in users of the roads exerting sufficient pressure on the trusts to ensure a good standard of upkeep and repair being maintained.

Although the new turnpikes provided for the main roads, the other highways were still maintained by the Surveyors appointed by the Vestry meeting every year. For their labour they relied on a very old Act passed in the reign of Philip and Mary which ordered all inhabitants to work for six days every year on the highways ; later amending legislation provided for a substitute instead of personal attendance, laid down the day's work as one of eight hours and required all occupiers of land to supply one cart and two able men. The Surveyor of the Highway had to inspect all roads three times each year, and defects were often announced in Church after the Sunday service, together with the days on which the Statute labour would be required.

The Justices had power to present any parish that neglected to maintain its roads in good order, failure to carry out the duties could result in a heavy fine.

The question of public or private roads sometimes cropped up, as the following resolution passed by the Vestry meeting held in Cranbrook on January 22, 1737 shows: " Agreed that as inconvenience and damage have occurred to the parish by Surveyors of Highways repairing private ways leading to particular people's lands that for the future no Surveyor be allowed anything for repairing private lanes or roads."

The Napoleonic wars at the end of the 18th century brought a rise in the cost of living without any corresponding increase in earnings, unemployment and distress in the country districts grew steadily more serious, and little effort to solve the problem could be detected in most rural areas.

It is greatly to the credit of the people of Cranbrook that they did attempt a solution that would employ the surplus labour in a manner to the advantage both of the men themselves and the general body of ratepayers.

With this purpose in view they hired, first Friezley and 70 acres of land, and later Sissinghurst Castle farm with its 300 or more acres. Work could be had by the able-bodied men of the parish who were otherwise unable to earn their living, especially during the winter months, and although the wages paid were low, they were sufficient to allow them to live without falling into the state of sullen despair common to the majority of the agricultural labouring class, compelled to exist on the meagre relief that the overseers in many parishes paid to them.

The experiment turned out a success, at times work was found for more than one hundred men on the farm, and the financial results were so favourable that Sissinghurst Castle farm continued to be managed by trustees appointed by the parish long after the emergency had passed; when the lease was finally given up in 1857 the credit balance of £3,700 provided the money with which to build the new Vestry Hall.

CHAPTER XII

THE NINETEENTH CENTURY

*" There methinks would be enjoyment more than in this
    march of mind,*
*In the steamship, in the railway, in the thoughts that
    shake mankind."*
—Tennyson.

The first forty years of the nineteenth century were a
time of steady progress for Cranbrook, from a population of
2,500 in 1801 there was an increase to 4,000 in 1841 and the
town enjoyed a period of prosperity such as it had not
experienced for two hundred years.

" A brief account of Cranbrook the Capital Town in the
Weald of Kent," published in 1815, has the following
description of the town :—

" The town of Cranbrook, or as it was originally spelt
Cranebrooke, is situate within the Weald of Kent, and from
the peculiarity of its situation forms the centre of an extensive
circle, and is also become the centre of its trade, which
considering its inland situation is by no means inconsiderable.
It contains many handsome private houses and the shops and
warehouses which are numerous and respectable are well
furnished. Here are also several respectable Inns, the chief
and most ancient of which is the George Inn, which was an
Inn prior to the reign of Queen Mary. The pursuer of
intellectual acquirements will also be gratified in finding an
extensive Library, containing a well chosen selection. The
town consists of two streets of considerable length meeting
at right angles, with a neat octagonal Market House at their
junction.

" The Market (which was obtained by Archbishop
Peckham in the 18th year of Edward I) is held on Saturdays,
at which considerable business is transacted in the sale of corn
and hops, particularly the latter, for which commodity it

holds the chief market in the Weald of Kent ; it is also well supplied with fish, of which great quantities are brought from the neighbouring sea ports, particularly from Hastings, and sold at a very reasonable rate. There are also two fairs for hops, corn, cattle and pedlary . . .

" For the salubrity of its air and the longevity of its inhabitants, Cranbrook stands unrivalled . . .

The road and footways . . . are now kept in good order, indeed no place in the Weald of Kent has undergone a greater revolution within the last 30 years than Cranbrook, and it still seems in a progressive state of improvement. It is pleasantly situated, being interspersed on every side with frequent hill and dale. The lands in general are very fertile, and adjoining to the town there are some very rich pastures, intermixed with arable land exceeding kindly to hops, the plantation of which in this parish is considered to be the largest in any parish in England.

A Stage Coach from the George Inn, Cranbrook, to the George Inn, Borough (through Maidstone) every Sunday, Tuesday and Thursday morning at 10 o'clock. A Stage Wagon from Cranbrook every Monday to the Talbot Inn, Borough, Southwark."

This contemporary account of Cranbrook, written in the year that witnessed the Battle of Waterloo and the final overthrow of Napoleon, calls for little comment. The writer, T. D. W. Dearn, architect, surveyor, author of the " Weald of Kent " and a local resident, expresses satisfaction at the present and perfect confidence in the future of his native town. There were good grounds for holding these optimistic views, farming was doing well and prices were good ; houses being built or rebuilt in the town and outside ; a new brewery had opened at Bakers Cross ; Humphreys the millwright had just put up a new windmill on The Hill (furnishing a landmark that happily is still there) ; William Tooth from his new hat factory off Stone Street supplied Cranbrook and the neighbourhood with his renowned beaver hats ; the Rope Walk, the hop sacking and Milkhouse Thread made at Milkhouse Street, tanners, braziers, printers, peruke makers, and a bank were all witnesses of the prosperity of the town.

Not everyone participated in these good times, in particular the agricultural labourer found it hard to exist on the meagre wages ; the peace that followed the long war against France made matters much worse for him and he often had to apply for parish relief to enable a bare existence to be maintained.

The parish farm at Sissinghurst Castle, providing, as it did work for the unemployed, prevented much hardship in Cranbrook, but in most parishes conditions got steadily worse until there broke out a serious outburst of rioting and disorder in the South Eastern counties of England in 1830.

Many feared a Revolution, special constables were sworn in, to guard ricks and barns which were being singled out for destruction by the unruly mobs.

In church, the Vicar of Cranbrook appealed to farmers to pay their men at least 2s. 6d. a day (an increase of 6d. a day on current wages). Crowds of men, often several hundreds in number, marched round the villages shouting their demands and destroying machinery, especially threshing machines, to which they partly attributed their distress.

In the absence of any regular police force, it became necessary to draft troops into the disaffected areas, and a troop of Dragoons came to Cranbrook, from whence they patrolled the neighbourhood ; a few arrests were made and eventually the trouble quietened down, not before much damage had been done in various parts of Kent and Sussex, but without any serious incident in Cranbrook.

Apart from this isolated outburst of violence there were other disturbing factors in the years after the war ; the failure of the local bank—Argylls, Bishop & Co., " The Weald of Kent Bank "—resulted in financial loss to the town. The bank notes of this firm, worthless although they are, often turn up as curiosities in the hands of local people whose family connections go back thus far.

The period witnessed much speculation in land ; a severe fall in values ruined a number of the speculators, with consequent reactions to the economy of the town. Despite these setbacks the general picture was one of continual progress and a moderate degree of prosperity. Possibly the outstanding impression one gets of the town in the 1830's is the feeling of self sufficiency ; it is true that further improvements to the roads had improved communications again—it was possible to go to London and back in one day by the Liberty coach at a return fare of 24s.—yet the shops of the town furnished most of the needs, and local interests occupied the minds of the dwellers in Cranbrook very largely to the exclusion of events in the world outside.

Thus the death of George IV in 1830 was marked by the tolling of the bells, but the proclamation of William IV five days later on July 20 roused great interest, being linked with the local personalities taking part in the proceedings. We read that Sam Dobell read the proclamation, George Dadson as high constable lead the procession around the town proclaiming the King at five points, and finally that " beer was given away "; thus did Cranbrook set the seal of its approbation on the new monarch.

But a change in the fortune of the town loomed ahead when in 1842 the railway line from London opened for traffic from Staplehurst station. At first the new venture received unqualified approval, for no-one could foresee that it could be anything but a benefit to the town.

Accustomed to road travel on the new turnpike roads, a mere six miles to the railway to take a train did not inconvenience the early enthusiasts, indeed a new turnpike road to link Hastings with Staplehurst was constructed, as it appeared that the engineering difficulties were too great to allow the railway to be extended from Tonbridge to Hastings ; a fast coach connected the town with the up train in the morning and returned to Hastings with passengers from London in the evening ; in addition a wagon for heavy goods and merchandise made the journey daily. For the same reason the new Benenden road from Golford to Farningham enabled the owner of Hemsted, Thomas Law Hodges, Member of Parliament, to travel to the station more comfortably and in less time.

The effects of the railway were not at first apparent, but by the 1850's the falling off in the attendance at the annual fairs had become noticeable, whilst the market—changed from Saturday to alternate Tuesdays early in the century— continued to fall away. The increase in machine-produced articles of all kinds began to compete with the output of local craftsmen, imported flour or wheat ground at the ports reduced the customers for the millers, hats, clothes, boots and shoes, pots and pans, all were made in the large manufacturing centres.

The population again began slowly to decline, agriculture fell away owing to the increased imports of foodstuffs, emigration to Canada offered inducements to the labourer and little by little the town relapsed into a quiet country village lying outside, and apart from that bustle and expansion the late Victoria era brought to many places.

In an attempt to arrest the decline, many efforts were made to obtain a direct railway connection—one project actually surveyed and mapped would have brought a branch line from between Marden and Staplehurst into the centre of the town with the station at the end of Carriers Road.

Another plan proposed a line from Paddock Wood following the course later taken by the existing branch, but instead of going to Hawkhurst it followed the Crane valley, with a suggested station near Bakers Cross, and then on to join the main line nearer to Ashford.

The Paddock Wood-Hawkhurst branch line finally opened in 1892, leaving Cranbrook town almost two miles distant from its station.

The steady fall in the importance of Cranbrook continued into the present century, but the advent of the motor car and motor bus, together with a more prosperous agricultural outlook, have brought new life back to the town in recent years.

CHAPTER XIII

THE CHURCH OF ST. DUNSTAN

*" And would my luckie fortune so much grace me
As in low Cranbrook or high Brenchley's hill."*

—Phineas Fletcher.

The parish church of St. Dunstan is a noble building in which is enshrined much of the history of the past. The church of to-day is mainly 15th and 16th century construction, but it stands on the site of two or three earlier buildings.

There are no records by which to determine the date of the first church in Cranbrook—one is mentioned towards the end of the eleventh century—but there are good reasons for supposing that this was built between 1030 and 1060 A.D. The land on which this church stood is part of the Dene of Cranbrook, then owned by Christ Church, Canterbury. The dedication to St. Dunstan, canonised in 1029, the unlikelihood of such a dedication after the Norman conquest, and the fact that Ethelnoth, Archbishop of Canterbury, 1020-1038, had been a monk of Dunstan's Abbey of Glastonbury, point to the conclusion that the church was built by his orders some time between 1029 and 1038.

There are no traces of Saxon work in the present building, but these early churches were usually of timber construction in isolated districts such as the Weald ; all signs of their existence would be lost when a more permanent stone church came to be built on the site. Such a stone building appears to have arisen in Cranbrook at some period during the 12th century. At the west end of the present church examination reveals a blocked doorway with rounded arch, partly covered by the last pillar on the south side of the nave, which is probably a fragment of this late Norman church.

The church we see to-day is a direct reminder of the sudden increase in prosperity and population that followed

Sir John Baker of Sissinghurst
(c. 1488-1558)

*Sissinghurst Castle in 1812, when in the occupation of the
Parish Authorities as a Workhouse*

The Tower of Sissinghurst Castle, about 1910

Upper High Street and the first Meeting House of the Quakers

the introduction of cloth making to Cranbrook ; the tower, south porch, chancel arch and part of the north aisle all having been completed before 1425. Work continued through most of the century ; in 1480 the eastern end of the north aisle is mentioned in a will bequeathing " 13s. 4d. to the newe worke of the north side of the churche."

In 1520 the work of rebuilding the middle aisle and raising the clerestory was undertaken ; a list of subscribers dated April 5, 1520, " to the new building of the middle aisle " reveals that a total of £247 had been collected, and a second list the following year records a further £120 paid towards the cost.

The enlargement of the chancel and an extension of the eastern end followed about thirty years later ; rebuilding the middle aisle and the addition of the clerestory had resulted in the south aisle being widened by three feet, which left the chancel arch " out of centre."

The interior of the church gives a pleasant impression of spaciousness and light derived from the colour of the stone-work and the clear glass of the clerestory windows.

At one time there must have been a considerable quantity of stained glass of mediæval origin ; in 1573 the church-wardens were cited for " reformation of the glass windows," and in 1583 an entry in the churchwardens' accounts records the payment of 15s. 4d. to the glazier " for mending the windows and taking down of pictures in the said windows," this after they had again been cited to appear at Canterbury for non-compliance with previous instructions. Some of this glass may have been preserved and later placed back in the east window, for in " A brief historical Account of Cranbrook " it is stated that " The east window is full of fine stained glass, many of the figures of it being entire and richly ornamented as to their drapery. There are several shields of arms remaining in it, among which are those of Wilsford, Guldeford quartered with Halden, within the Order of the Garter, and archbishop Bouchier, being those of the See of Canterbury."

Dearn writes in 1815: " The great east window contains much stained glass, some of the figures of which are entire, but being for the most part made up of small pieces, nothing like design is to be traced in it."

All this glass was removed in 1861 when considerable alterations were made to the interior of the church and a memorial to the Tooth family, in the form of a modern stained glass window took its place.

The old glass, after being stored away for a number of years, eventually found a new resting place in a window of the north aisle, unfortunately pieces were lost or broken and little of the original design is preserved.

There have been many changes to the interior of the church in the course of the years, the collapse of a pillar of the south aisle in 1725 as a result of opening the Baker vault for a burial, led to the roof of the nave being lowered, the oak being covered in with a plaster ceiling ; when the extensive alterations of 1866 were being carried out this ceiling being removed it became apparent that the roof had so decayed that a complete renewal was necessary, the present roof is claimed to be an exact replica of the original.

In 1755 the Vestry meeting agreed that " a gallery be built as useful and commodious as may be." This gallery is often referred to and especial pride is displayed in " a fine piece of painting at the back thereof which consists of two fluted columns with ornamental capitals ; around an eliptical arch is the representation of a crimson curtain with drapery of ermine and bordered with gold fringed lace, it is formed into six festoons from each of which is pendant a gold cord with tassels and finished at the top with a Crown which reaches to the ceiling ; within the arch is placed the King's arms elegantly carved in wood and splendidly gilt. On each side of the arms is a window painted in form of those round the church, through which is represented a cloudy sky in perspective." Alas for this artistic masterpiece of the 18th century, it was lost when the gallery disappeared during the mid-Victorian alterations.

The ceiling of the chancel painted in various colours was adorned " with four hollow pieces of carving, gilt, and the border underneath contains paintings of Cherubims, Crowns and Sceptres."

The " four hollow pieces of carving " were the curious old carved oak bosses now displayed on the wall at the west end, and are judged to be 14th century work ; they were removed from the roof of the chancel during the restoration of the church already mentioned.

There are several unusual features to be noted in Cranbrook church ; the dipping font for baptism by total immersion is unique in the county and rarely to be found elsewhere. This was built by the Vicar, the Rev. John Johnson, in 1710 for the purpose of overcoming the objections of the Baptists who were then numerically very strong in the parish. By providing facilities for adult baptism by dipping he hoped to persuade them to rejoin the Anglican church, his efforts met with little success and only one such adult baptism is recorded in the registers.

A second uncommon feature is the remarkable monument on the south wall to the Roberts family.

It recounts the geneology of the family for nearly four hundred years and was erected at the direction of Jane, Duchess of St. Albans, the last of the family in the direct line. The knowledge of the unhappiness of her marriage with the Duke has prompted the thought that this elaborate recital of the pedigree of the family offered a more solid foundation for family pride than the ducal splendour her husband derived from his descent from the natural son of Charles II and Nell Gwyn.

There are few brasses in the church, the oldest one is on the stone of Thomas Sheafe, who died in 1520. This depicts a merchant in his robes and an infant child with the initials T.S. and his cloth mark in the centre ; indents on other stones indicate the presence at one time of more 15th and 16th century brasses but they have long since disappeared.

When Queen Elizabeth visited Cranbrook in 1573 she was welcomed with a cheerful ringing of the bells in the tower of the church ; there were then five and they were a source of worry and expense to the churchwardens for years— recast in 1715 into six, it was found that three of them would not ring—so they were again recast, into eight this time, continuing in service until 1800, when a new set of eight bells by Mears was purchased. These were rehung in 1812 by Humphrey the millwright, who was engaged at this time in building the new mill on The Hill, reports indicate that the work done to the frame gave general satisfaction.

In addition to the bells, the tower also held the Chimes. Installed in 1572, their music rang out every three hours for nearly three hundred years until they were removed in 1845 after an inspection had revealed that the mechanical connections of the hammer work were in a very dilapidated condition, whilst the obsolete principle upon which the barrel and barrel frame were constructed precluded any repair. Nevertheless the Vestry meeting passed a resolution that " it was expedient to have new chimes" and appointed a committee to carry out the resolution. There the matter ended, for the new chimes were never installed, but whether the loss of this regular repetition of musical notes proved to be a loss or a gain must be left to the choice of the individual townsman.

A list of the Rectors and Vicars, compiled by the Rev. T. S. Frampton, contains almost sixty names. The first Rector, Gaufridus Forti, styled Dean of Cranbrook, may have been the Rural Dean of the Charing Deanery, in 1177, not yet divided in East and West. William de Mepham, 1310, was the last of the Rectors, for in 1332 the Archbishop who had hitherto owned the advowson, from now on enjoyed the appropriation of the rectory, together with the advowson of the vicarage instituted and endowed at this time. This arrangement continued in force until the primacy of Archbishop Cranmer, who exchanged the appropriation of the rectory with Henry VIII, retaining the advowson of the vicarage. By a charter dated May, 1543, the King settled the appropriation of the rectory on the newly-founded Dean and Chapter of Canterbury.

Robert de Walsham, who made a remarkable number of changes within a very limited time, was Vicar for eighteen weeks in 1376, exchanging for Little Chart.

He was Confessor to the Black Prince and is mentioned in his will.

The most noteworthy occupant of the benefice was Hugh ap Rice or Hugh Price, 1533-1554. Born in Brecon in 1495, he was educated at the well-known monastery of Oxeney, near Oxford, graduating at the University there in 1512. Appointed to Cranbrook by Archbishop Cranmer, Dr. Price (Doctor of Canon Law, 1526), nominated Prebendary of Rochester in 1541 on the creation of the Dean and Chapter, retained the vicarage of Cranbrook until the accession of Queen Mary.

Soon after Queen Elizabeth ascended the throne, Dr. Price submitted a petition for the grant of the site of an existing hostel at Oxford for the purpose of founding a college where it would be possible for his fellow countrymen to have a recognized home and associate together as a community. Letters Patent founding Jesus College, Oxford, were issued in 1571, and in the same year he received the appointment of Treasurer of St. David's.

A portrait of Dr. Price attributed to the School of Holbein is in the possession of Jesus College. This was engraved by George Vertue in 1739 and for many years a copy of the engraving was given to every scholar of the College. Dr. Price died in 1576.

An alabaster tablet on the north wall of the chancel records Richard Fletcher, Vicar of Cranbrook, 1558-1585. He had two sons ; Richard, Vicar of Rye, 1573, after Dean of Peterborough, in which office he attended Mary Queen of Scots at her execution, Bishop of Bristol and Bishop of London ; he married as his second wife the widow of Sir Richard Baker of Sissinghurst to the great displeasure of the Queen ; his only son by his first marriage, John Fletcher, is the well-known collaborator with Beaumont. The second son, Dr. Giles Fletcher (whose assistance the parish had solicited in the controversy with Lydd on the question of coast watching) was later Ambassador to Russia and author of an early book on that country.

CHAPTER XIV

THE PARISH REGISTERS

The parish registers start in 1559 ; an instruction to
" provide a faire register booke, wherein they shall register
all cristenynges, burialls and mariages, and also the
accomptes of the churche and the same to be kept under
lock and keye " issued after a Visitation in 1557 suggests that
the order of Thomas Cromwell for registers to be kept in all
parishes had not been complied with in Cranbrook. The
parchment register opens with the following paragraph on
the title page:

" This Register is divided into three bookes in the which
are conteined the names of all such persons which have bene
either Baptised, Married and Buryed within the parrish of
Cranbrooke from yeare to yeare and from tyme to tyme which
Register was begun to be keapte in the moneth of August
A.D. 1559. Theye were ffirst writen in a booke of paper
appointed for that purpose and so contynued from the yeare
above writen unto the ffirst day of December A.D. 1598, at
which tyme all that was writen before untill then were taken
out of the sayed book of Paper and placed into this Booke of
Parchment by commandemente from authoritie for the better
continuance of the same unto Posteritie. The Pastor or
minister then of the parrish of Cranbrooke was William Eddye
A.M. of the universitie of Cambridge and borne in the Cittie
of Bristoll whoe wroat or coppied out this Register to the end
it might more faithfullie be donne with his owne hand."

In 1597/8 an outbreak of the plague in the parish carried
off nearly two hundred people, and the Vicar made a note of
this in the Register:

" In this year followinge 1597, began the great plague
in Cranbrooke, the which continued from April the yeare
aforesaide unto the 13th of July 1598.

1. It is to be observed that before this infection did
begin, that God, about a year or two before, took away by
death many honest and good men and women.

78

2. That the judgement of God for sin, was much before threatened, and specially for that vice of drunkeness which did abounde heare.

3. That this infection was in all quarters at that time of this parish except Hartley quarter.

4. That the same began in the house of one Brighteling, out of which much thievery was committed, and that it ended in the house of one Henry Crynnocke, who was a pott companion, and his wife noted much for incontinence, which both died excommunicated.

5. That this infection was gotte almost into all the inns and sutling houses in the town, places then of greate misorder, so that God did seem to punish himself which officers did neglect and not regard.

6. Together with this infection, there was a greate dearth at the same tyme, which was cause also of much heavyness and sorrow.

7. This was most grievous unto me of all, that this judgment of God did not draw people unto repentance the more, but that many by it seemed the more hardened in theyre sin.

Will: Eddy.

" Now also this year others of the plague who were buried near to their several dwellings, because they could get none to carry them unto the church, for it was in the begininge of this infection, so that none would venture themselves. The certain day of their burials one could not learn." Then follow the names and places of burial.

The second register starts from 1653—it was a Civil register ordered by an Act of Parliament.

" According to an Act of Parliament in that behalf made, choise hath been made by the Major part of the Inhabitants of the parish of Cranbrook in the County of Kent (chargeable to the relief of the poor) of John Butcher of Cranbrook aforesaid to be parish register of the parish aforesaid of whom we Thomas Plumer and John Rabson Esquires two Justices of the Peace of the said County doe approve . . . ."

This register was well kept and contains much more information than had hitherto been furnished in the earlier one. It is a source of regret that this practise of supplying details of parentage, occupation and residence should have been abandoned when the Register reverted to the care of the Vicar after the Restoration.

The third register, divided into separate books, has an account of some of the Vicars of Cranbrook on the inside of the front cover of the register of Baptisms. This information was inserted by the Rev. John Johnson, and is prefaced by the following paragraph:

"His Grace William (Wake. Th.) Archbishop of Canterbury did at the request of John Johnson Vicar of Cranbrook administer Confirmation at this place to above thirteen hundred persons, of which one third at least were of this parish, on Sunday Jan. 24th A.D. 1716. There had been no confirmation here in 28 years before, that is, since the fatal year 1688, when the most Reverend Abp. Sancroft of pious memory being discharged from his custody in the Tower upon a Trial in the Kings Bench, sent Bishop Leving (of Man) to perform the office of Confirmation thr'out the diocese, as he did Bishop Lloyd (of Norwich) some years before.

The same Archbishop of his own free Motion again administered Confirmation here on Sunday June 21st 1724 to above thirteen hundred persons, as his Chaplain who attended him in the office, told me: yet one of his Grace's Liverymen, who said he numbered them all, affirmed to me that they were but twelve hundred."

Following the appointment of the Rev. John Johnson in 1707 we again find valuable information in these registers, for he not only notes the trades, professions and conditions of his parishioners, following the practice of Commonwealth times ; he also marks as dissenters all those burials of persons not members of the Anglican Church, adding the remark: "They were buried without giving notice to the Vicar." The Quakers had many members in Cranbrook in the 18th century, they had their own burial ground just outside the town at Courtstile and the registers have a note, "at the Quakers burying place" or "ground" in recording the burial of one of their number.

As with all parish registers, much of the history that lies embedded in their pages is a valuable source of information and confirmation of events and happenings now almost forgotten:

Richard Fox of Bedgebury Furnace (Furnace Farm), furnaceman, buried in 1655, shows that the iron furnace was working as late as this year.

Bernard Woolett, a smuggler shot in Goudhurst churchyard, buried 1746, recalls the fight between the Hawkhurst gang of smugglers and the people of Goudhurst.

John Johnson, a militia soldier, shot by accident at Sissinghurst, buried 1759.

William Barruck, killed by a French prisoner at Sissinghurst, buried 1761, are two entries that bring back to mind the days of Sissinghurst Castle as a prisoner of war camp, as do these entries from the register of marriages in 1762 : —

Laurence Calberte, a prisoner among the French at Sissinghurst House, and Mary Pepper.

Michael Chapron, a prisoner at Sissinghurst, and Elizabeth Godfrey.

The burial of Elizabeth Paine, wife of Thomas Paine (author of the " Rights of Man," " Age of Reason," etc.) in 1808, records a little known connection between Cranbrook and this stormy revolutionary of the 18th century.

Tom Paine, then an Excise officer stationed at Lewes, met and married as his second wife, Elizabeth Ollive, daughter of a tobacconist in that town.

The marriage did not turn out a happy one, and after three years, a deed of separation was agreed upon. Mrs. Paine came to Cranbrook to live with her brother, Thomas Ollive, a clockmaker and silversmith of repute, where she remained until her death.

Paine kept up a correspondence with his wife, and died a few months after her in New York, from whence years later Cobbett brought his bones back to England, where they were detained by the Customs at Liverpool and their subsequent fate is obscure.

CHAPTER XV

THE PARISH MEETING

" Where village statesmen talked with looks profound
And news much older than the ale went round."

—Goldsmith.

Democracy is a word that is often on the tongue in modern speech. It is sometimes understood as giving everyone the right to air their opinions on any question of national or local government on condition that no personal liability or responsibility is incurred.

This widely held attitude of mind is partly the result, and also partly the reason for the increasing tendency towards centralization and the growth of bureaucratic control, and is a far cry from those days when local administration and government were the business of each parish and its inhabitants.

A rural community existed largely as a self-supporting unit, economically and politically, and, subject to the general oversight of the Justices of the Peace, all the orders and instructions of the central government had to be interpreted and carried out in each parish by officers appointed by the parish meeting. These officials were as numerous as the duties they were called upon to perform ; Churchwardens, Sidesmen, Surveyors of the Highway, Overseers of the Poor, Borsholder or Head Constable, and other minor posts were all filled by the ordinary people in rotation. Much of the success of the early settlements in New England can be attributed to the training in local self-government that were brought from English villages by the early colonists.

The early records for Cranbrook extend back to the first Churchwarden book commencing in 1558, the last year of Phillip and Mary. Later came the Rate Books (a fragment for the years 1610-15, regularly from 1680 onwards), the Overseers' Accounts, Vestry Minute Books, Highway Accounts, Parish Farm Records and other miscellaneous items, all of which have recently been deposited at the Archives Office of the County Council at Maidstone.

When Uniformity became the law of the land in the reign of Queen Elizabeth I, it was a logical sequence to entrust the details of local administration to the congregation assembled at the annual church meeting, when the office-holders for the ensuing year were appointed. The practice of holding the position of churchwarden for two years was always followed in Cranbrook, the senior warden retiring on completing this term, whilst the junior warden took his place and nominated a new candidate for the approval of the assembly, to become in turn the senior warden the following year.

The accounts for these early years are minutely detailed and present a vivid picture of the many petty items that required attention—whitewashing the church, mending the glass in the windows, keeping pigs out of the churchyard, recasting the bells, selling the old vestments and other furniture no longer required, " buying a piece of white cloth to mend the surplice of Mr. Vicar $2\frac{1}{2}$d.," appointing assessors for the " church scott " and collectors to gather the same, and a host of similar matters.

Then there were legal questions to be resolved ; the long dispute with Symon Lynch over the School dragged on for a number of years before an agreement could be negotiated ; a libel by a certain John Sandes which the parish asked Sir Richard Baker to defend, " Dr. Lakes legal charges 13s. 8d." and "Expenses riding to Canterbury and dinner for Sir Richard Baker and Dr. Lake, 12s. 8d."; a citation to appear at Canterbury for not removing the painted " images from the windows." (A painter had been ordered to paint over the glass to cover them up, but this did not meet with the approval of the Archdeacon, who cited the churchwardens and sidesmen, eventually they had to be removed by a glazier and plain glass substituted).

Until the dispute with Symon Lynch had been settled, the parish assumed responsibility for the School, doing repairs to the building, which included new floors and " loks and thymbles for the scholehouse gate, 1s.," but after the settlement the parish ceased to have any part in the affairs of the School. Shortly afterwards, however, with the foundation of Dence's School, we again find them concerned with educational business, the control of this school continued to be exercised by the Parish meeting for many years.

So far the greater part of the work of the churchwardens related to church matters, it often involved them in financial expenditure that was not always repaid immediately—there were cases where it had not been found possible for the parish to pay the debt due to a churchwarden for a year and more after he left office ; with the introduction of new legislation relating to the care of the poor and upkeep of roads, it became necessary to appoint parish officers charged with the carrying out of these further responsibilities.

The Vestry Minute Books from 1700 onwards deal with a bewildering variety of subjects, as may be deduced from the extracts now quoted.

Dec. 8, 1706.   Agreed in vestry that Peter Allen shall be sent to be confined in Bedlam.

Dec. 7, 1707.   John Groombridge M.A., John Leigh senr. gent, Jacob Hollingsworth gent, Jacob Walter gent, Isaac Walter gent, and John Weston gent, are desirous of more convenient sittings in the church their request is conceded to by their being at the expense of making their own pews.

Oct. 17, 1714.   Agreed that Saml. Harman should build a new chimney to the Writing School (Dence's School).

Apl. 19, 1715.   Agreed that five bells should be cast into six.

March 6, 1719.   Agreed to allow Chas. Taylor £3 towards putting his son William apprentice to Henry Butler.

Apl. 10, 1720.   Agreed to allow Stephen Smith of Staplehurst £10 for his expense and trouble in getting James Scotchford in Bedlam. If he don't accept of that he shall have nothing.

Dec. 9, 1722.   The present officers shall Hire a House for the poor or a workhouse for employing the poor.

Oct. 6, 1728.   Agreed to stand by the late Overseers in their distress that they make upon Mr. Daniel Tilden for the Poor Cess due to the Parish the last two years.

June 21, 1730.   Agreed to allow the Wardens £5 per cent interest on £183 that they are out of pocket until they be paid.

May 6, 1733. Agreed that whereas Hawkhurst nor Goudhurst pay for no hedgehog neither are of opinion that they do any hurt therefore we order the Churchwardens to pay for no more after this day.

Nov. 24, 1741. Agreed to sue the Parish Officers of Maidstone on a note of hand. Charges due to the Parish of Cranbrook for allowing Stephen Pemble to have the Small Pox in their Parish.

Sept. 18, 1743. Upon a full hearing in Vestry in relation to the Affidavit made for Josiah Bowles deceased which was not delivered to Mr. Disney in due time pursuant to the Act for burying in Woollen. The same appearing to be owing to the neglect of the person who made the same and no fraud intended we do hereby agree to remit the Penalty thereon.

Apl. 22, 1744. Agreed that Mr. John Beckett shall be Apothecary to the Workhouse for the year ensuing.

March 24, 1745. Agreed that the Parishioners shall not be obliged to work six working days (on the roads) as has formerly been usual in this parish but the Surveyors shall employ such persons as they shall adjudge most Proper, and further no person shall pay more than 10s. for not working the whole six days and not less than 1s. 6d. for the present year.

Sept. 25, 1748. Agreed to sue on all bonds to indemnify the Parish against (the charge for) Bastard children the Obligors having refused to perform their conditions.

Dec. 3, 1749. Agreed to take a Dividend with other Creditors in relation to what is due to the Parish from Mr. Adams.

Sept. 9, 1750. Whereas the late Rev. Mr. R. Elsworth by his Will gave Two pounds yearly to be laid out by the Minister of Cranbrook for Books, now we at a Vestry held this day do order that the Churchwardens for the time being or their successors do take proper methods for recovery of same at the charge and expense of the parish.

Oct. 23, 1757. Agreed Respecting the Question whether the Vicar's Tithes are paid at Easter for the past or present year the following parishioners declare they believe it to be for the present year.

July 16, 1762. Agreed that the Money to be paid by the Churchwardens and Overseers to such persons as shall be enrolled in the Militia for this parish to be paid out of the Poor Tax without making a Tax on purpose.

June 11, 1765. Agreed that the pavement of the road 100 yards distant of St. Davids Bridge belongs to the constable of the Hundred and not to the Parish, and that the Surveyor shall indict the same at next Quarter Sessions. Also that the late Churchwardens pay over the balance they hold to the present Wardens within a month of this date and in future all Wardens, Overseers and Surveyors pay over their balances within a month of going out of office in default thereof to be presented to the Justices or the Ecclesiastical Court as the case shall require.

Jan. 18, 1767. We, the inhabitants of the Parish of Cranbrook in the County of Kent this day assembled in Vestry do absolutely deny that any Persons under Enochelation (Vaccination) shall have any use of the Pest House.

1772. Church Porch. It appears the timbers are much decayed, it is therefore ordered that the present sharp roof be taken down and to be repaired with a flat roof with stone battlements round it to make it uniform.

Feb. 18, 1780. Agreed to purchase two fire Hooks and a Leather pipe to be paid from Poor Rate.

June 8, 1781. Agreed to borrow £150 for the relief of the Poor, the Churchwardens and Overseers to give the joint Note of Hand as security.

Jan. 20, 1786. A Vestry to consider the demand of 13 years arrears composition money made by the Trustees of Tenterden Turnpike. It was resolved in the negative.

June 21, 1798. At this Vestry complaint was made that the rating in the Parish was very unequal. Two persons appointed for a revaluation. J. A. Walter of Marden and H. Kingsnorth of Kennardington. The cost to be paid out of the Rates.

Parish relief for the poor and sick imposed a heavy charge on the ratepayers and every effort was made to lighten the burden, thus we find the Vestry Meeting in 1723 agreeing " to pay John Russell, butcher of Milkhouse, £10 to enable him to go forward in his business and so prevent his family from becoming chargeable on the parish, but only on the express condition that his father in law, John Bridgland, discharge all his debts.

The earliest rate book is dated 1608, but unfortunately those for the years 1612-1675 are lost and 1676-1685 are badly mutilated. From 1687 onwards the rate books and the overseers' accounts are complete, affording much information and insight into the finances and local administration of a typical rural community.

In 1687 a Poor Rate of 2s. 6d. in the pound brought in £429 2s., all of which was spent in relief. Orphan children were boarded out with other families, sums ranging from 6s. to 14s. a month being paid for their support. Grants were made to more than 50 families to enable them to pay their rents, whilst over 60 old people and widows received monthly payments in cash varying from 2s. to 8s. a month.

Medical treatment is recorded in very general terms:

" Paid Richard Hope for the cure of William Wildish his leg £2 5s. 6d., and for what he did to Goodman Hopkins 3s. 6d."

" Paid Dr. Groombridge for phisick for Widow Peene 4s. 6d."

" Paid to the Mountebanke for stuff for Susan Lye's eyes 4s."

" Paid Richard Hope, Barber Chirugeon towards George Jarvis, his legs 10s., and for John Portwith's child hand being burnt 12s."

Clothing figures regularly among the payments:

" For Will Wildish 2 shirts 4s. and a payre of hoose and shoose 4s. 8d."

" A bed, bolster, payre of sheets, coverlet, and blanket for Thos. Colville 17s."

" Mantel and petty coat for Colvilles girl (at Borners) 10s."

" $3\frac{1}{2}$ yards Kersey to make Ric. Martin's coat 8s. 2d."

" Wastecote for Old Morris 4s. 9d."

" Pr. of Breeches for Old Hubbard 3s. 6d."

Other disbursments included such diverse items as:

" A warrant to cause young people to go to church 6s."

" A spade for old Gonre 2s."

" Woollen wheel for old Colbrooke's wife 2s. 6d."

" A tovet ($\frac{1}{2}$ bushel) of wheat for old Cook 2s. 2d."

" For mending Cripple Welsh's cart 3s. 6d."

"2 years Lords rent (quit rent) for John Bathurst 3s."

" Reparations about Lye's house 10s. 9d."

" Paid for clothes for Tolhurst's son going to service to the Lady Howard £2 14s. 3d."

" Paid by order of the Parish for relieving Simon Hewes out of prison £7."

" Paid Simon Hewes wife he being in jayle 14s."

These details have been selected to show the diverse methods by which the Overseers attempted to lighten the burdens of the poor in a manner both humane and just.

CHAPTER XVI

CRANBROOK SCHOOL

" Here I am in Kent and Christendome
Among the muses where I read and rhyme."

—Sir Thomas Wyatt.

The precise date of the foundation of the School at
Cranbrook cannot be stated with any degree of certainty—
there is mention of a schoolmaster in the Glassenbury rentals
of 1484—but the credit for the earliest endowment is due to
John Blubery, a yeoman of the King's Armoury in the reign
of Henry VII.

Whether Blubery was a native of Cranbrook is uncertain,
but he owned several properties in the parish and in his will
proved 22nd March, 1518, he directed " the chief mansion
place of my land to be at the disposicion of William Lynche
to founde a frescole howse for all the pour children of the
towne of Cranbrooke aforesaid, after the death of his wife,
and subject to the child of " my daughter if it be not a man
child." He further directed that the schoolmaster should be
chosen and appointed by William Lynch whom he made his
executor in conjunction with his wife, Joane Blubery.

How long Joane survived her husband has not been
established, but the property eventually passed into the
possession of William Lynch as directed.

William Lynch, a prosperous clothier who had married
a Hendley, died in 1539, and his property passed to his son
Simon, who had gone from Cranbrook to Sandwich, where he
became an important personage and represented the town in
Parliament ; whether the school had been established at
this time is not certain, the earliest documentary evidence is
found in the Churchwardens' accounts for the year 1560 which
contain items relating to certain repairs carried out at the
" scholehouse." It seems probable that the Blubery property
had been handed over for the uses designated in the will of
1518, but the endowment of the school had been further

89

increased by the gift of a farm at Horsemonden from William Lynch. This legacy did not receive specific mention in his will which does not deal with his landed property—this was probably settled by deeds of feoffment—and for some reason Simon Lynch refused to execute a conveyance of the property in accordance with the wishes of his father.

Legal proceedings were started against him by the parish and the law suit went on for more than two years, eventually being settled by a compromise whereby Simon Lynch should enjoy the benefit of a twenty-one year lease of the property, at the end of this period it would revert to the parish, and in 1564 Simon Lynch " for a certain consideration him thereunto moving " conveyed certain property to trustees for the perpetual maintenance of a grammar school at Cranbrook. This included the house called " Blewberryes " with garden adjoining, and also a farm at Horsemonden.

In 1573 Queen Elizabeth I visited Cranbrook when she graciously expressed her willingness to grant a Charter to the school ; to enable Her Majesty's wish to be speedily carried out, Simon Lynch voluntarily gave up to the parish his rights in the unexpired portion of the twenty-one years' lease granted to him in 1564.

The Charter bears the date of May 8th, 1574, and recites that Simon Lynch, son of William Lynch. of Cranbrook, doth propose to give and grant certain lands " according to the Intention of the aforesaid William Lynch his father for the perpetual support and maintenance of the same free Grammar School within the Parish of Cranbrook aforesaid. Know ye that We heartily desiring to promote the pious proposal aforesaid and also that the aforesaid free and perpetual Grammar School within the parish of Cranbrook may be brought to perfection firmly to endure for ever Of our special Grace . . . . Do for Us our Heirs and Successors Will and Grant that within the Parish of Cranbrook there shall hereafter be for ever a certain free and perpetual Grammar School and that the same school shall hereafter for ever be called the free and perpetual Grammar School of Queen Elizabeth in Cranbrook."

This original charter is still in the possession of the Governors and has recently been placed in a specially designed cabinet in Big School.

The first Governors were Richard Fletcher, Vicar of Cranbrook, Sir Richard Baker, Walter Roberts, Esq., Walter

Hendley, Esq., Thomas Sheaff, Peter Courthope, Robert Brickenden, Francis Hartridge, John Courthope, Thomas Rucke, Richard Hovenden, William Sheaff and Lawrence Sharpe. It is interesting to observe that the last named nine were all members of important families of clothiers. The charter provided that the Vicar of Cranbrook for the time being should always be a Governor of the School.

In the early days the school was of course a day school, masters were appointed and resigned at fairly frequent intervals, whilst the equipment appears to have been rudimentary to judge from the following inventory taken in 1666:—

" A full and just account of the utensils and appurtenances belonging to the Grammar School house of Queen Elizabeth in Cranbrook.

IN THE SCHOOL

1 Riders Dictionary.　　1 Scavula's Lexicon.
1 John Munkouse Dictionary.
2 Long Tables.　　3 Long forms.
3 Locks and Keys.　　2 Bolts with 3 Staples.

IN THE KITCHEN

1 Portall with iron latch and hatch in the Door.
1 Lock and Key with an Iron Knocker on the Street door.
1 Long bench and 1 short one.
1 Short dresser.　　1 short screen."

The first headmaster to hold the position for sufficient length of time to be able to establish a tradition in the school was the Rev. Thomas Crowther, of Ashford, appointed in October, 1689, and remaining until his death in January, 1740, a period of 50 years.

The Rev. Thomas Greenall, appointed in 1767, was succeeded in 1812 by his son-in-law, Rev. D. W. Davies, who continued as headmaster until his death in 1850.

During the headmastership of the Rev. Charles Crowden, 1866-1888 there were very considerable alterations and enlargements to the school and the number of boarders rose to 158. At this period no stipend was paid by the Governors, but they kept the buildings in repair, the Master having the use of them rent free, paying to the Governors a capitation fee for all boarders. The boarding fee of fifty guineas a year was retained by the Headmaster.

Under the 1946 Education Act the control of the school is now largely in the hands of the County Council, but the Governors still have many duties to perform, and the Foundation assets are entirely in their hands. The farm at Horsemonden was recently sold and the proceeds were invested in Government securities.

School House, a pleasing example of early Georgian architecture, built in the early part of the 18th century, stands on the site of the original " Blewberries."

The Governors' Board Room in School House is panelled in oak, the panelling is Tudor and came from Shepherds in the High Street.

When this latter house underwent considerable structural alterations about 100 years ago the panelling was removed and seemed likely to be used to build a pig pound, but fortunately it escaped this fate, being bought for about £5 and re-erected in School House.

There is a large table in the Governors' Room with a magnificent carved panel centre of Queen Elizabeth I. This was made for the Governors in 1723, the carving being done in the Navy Yard at Chatham. For many years it formed part of the furniture of the School farm at Horsemonden, where it was the custom for the Governors to hold their annual meeting, followed by a dinner supplied by the tenant of the farm for the time being.

CHAPTER XVII

SISSINGHURST

" But 'tis so lately alter'd that the old name
Is fresh about me."
—Henry VIII.

The ecclesiastical parish of Sissinghurst is quite modern, having been created about one hundred years ago to provide for the needs of the eastern portion of the parish of Cranbrook. It is made up from the village of Milkhouse Street and the districts of Golford, Three Chimneys and The Common, with a few other scattered areas. Milkhouse Street is probably the oldest settled portion of the whole parish of Cranbrook, being situated at the spot where the old Roman road crossed the track leading to the denes that formed part of the possessions of Little Chart and the Royal Manor of Wye; most of the village in fact arose on the dene of Karckeregge (Little Chart) or Lower Wilsley (Wye).

Although it has always been a part of the parish of Cranbrook, Milkhouse Street—the largest hamlet outside the town and nearly two miles away—from earliest times has developed on independent lines as a community apart.

It was in the year 1401 that Archbishop Arundel granted a licence " to those dwelling in the hamlet of Milkhouse within the parish of Cranbrook, that in the Chapel of Holy Trinity newly built within the hamlet of Milkhouse they may have Mass and other divine offices at suitable times by efficient chaplains."

This chapel stood on the corner of the road leading to Golford (still named Chapel Lane) and nearly opposite to the present church. It was suppressed in 1548 under the Act granting all Chantries, Free Chapels and Colleges to the Crown, although as a Chapel of Ease of St. Dunstan's, Cranbrook, it did not really come under any of these categories, but the purchaser of the lands that formed the endowment of the Chapel, Sir John Baker, was at that time the most important man in the parish with powerful influence at Court and any action likely to arouse his antagonism would have been very unwise.

Part of the ruins of the old chapel remained standing for nearly three hundred years after its suppression—the eastern end with the window being a favourite subject for artists of the late 18th and early 19th centuries.

The present Trinity Church was not built until the year 1838, and then almost by chance.

In 1824 Rear Admiral the Honourable James King purchased Angley on retiring from the Royal Navy. During his service he had escorted Louis XVIII to France, conveyed the Princess of Wales to Cuxhaven after her separation from the Prince Regent, and as captain of the frigate " Jason " had taken Lady Hester Stanhope on the first stage of her journey to the Near East. He married in 1815, Caroline, the second daughter of Euseby Cleaver, Archbishop of Dublin.

The seventh son of the Earl of Kingston, Admiral King had a sister Louisa who married Count De Spaen ; the only daughter of this marriage, Caroline, became the wife of the Rev. Henry O. Cleaver, Vicar of Hawkhurst, and a son of Archbishop Cleaver.

On the death of her husband, Mrs. Cleaver went to live with her mother at Wandsworth, but Lady Louisa, wishing to be near her brother in Cranbrook, they looked for a suitable place and eventually rented Swifts as a temporary home, in the meantime seeking a site on which they could build a house. Their choice fell on a piece of land on Milkhouse Heath where stood a row of old cottages, the property of the parish, in which old people had been allowed to live rent free, but no longer required for this purpose after the opening of the Union Workhouse.

Lady Louisa demolished the cottages, bought more of the land and built Camden Lodge, but before it was ready for occupation the death in 1842 of Philadelphia Nairn, last surviving member of the Plummer family, of Plummers Place, resulted in this property coming on to the market. It was bought by Lady Louisa, who proceeded to pull down the fine old timber framed Tudor House, and build on the site a new house which she called Sissinghurst Place.

Several years before all this housebuilding activity, Lady Louisa and her brother, the Admiral, had resolved to avail themselves of the opportunity afforded by the passing of an

Act of Parliament in the early years of the reign of William IV permitting the building of new churches in those parishes where they would be of use, and decided to erect a new church at Tubs Lake to serve the needs of the outlying parts of both Cranbrook and Hawkhurst. This was in 1833, a site was selected and Mr. J. Jennings, architect of Hawkhurst, received a commission to draw up the plans.

The project met with much opposition from the Rev. Cyril Hutchinson, Vicar of Hawkhurst, as the following extracts from letters he wrote to Dr. Bull, Treasurer of the Dean and Chapter of Canterbury, reveals.

" 15 Nov., 1833. The site is ill chosen as it is half in Hawkhurst and half out. The promoters are Evangelicals and the chief one is Capt. King, uncle of Mr. Cleaver. The new chapel is intended as an insidious attack on the parish of Hawkhurst. The clergyman at the proposed chapel will be able to pass over the boundaries of Cranbrook and Hawkhurst ' like a gypsy.' The chapel was negociated with absolute secrecy."

" 27 Nov., 1833. I have seen the Archbishop (Howley), who will not directly oppose the new chapel. I do not think the requirements of the Act of Parliament are fulfilled as over a third of the parishioners are accomodated at the parish church. Jennings is the architect, he belongs to a family of Dissenters who frequent chapel in the afternoon and church in the morning."

The opposition to the new church at Tubs Lake succeeded in halting the project, Admiral King received an invitation to call on the Archbishop and was told that it would be of greater benefit to build a new church at Milkhouse Street, and in any case " he positively and finally refused to allow the church to be built at Tubs Lake."

This setback to their plans did not daunt the promoters, although it somewhat delayed operations as it was necessary to obtain a suitable piece of ground on which a church could be built, but eventually Lord Cornwallis offered a portion of a field forming part of the Bull farm, and in February, 1837, Mr. Jennings received instructions to submit his plans as the church " was at length to be set about." It appears that the church of Casterton near Stamford formed the design from which these plans were prepared. Stone for building from the quarries of Lord Cornwallis and Mr. Law Hodges at Golford, and sand from the Angley pit of Admiral King were both given free of cost.

Tenders were invited and one for £1,335 from James Reed, builder, of Hawkhurst, received the contract, subject to the figure being reduced to £1,280, which Reed agreed to do, and the work started.

The construction went ahead rapidly, payments on account being made from time to time against the architect's certificate, but in March, 1838, the following letter came from the builder:—

" Sir,—I have already paid the whole of the amount which I received on account of the Church at Milkhouse Street, and collecting my bills find that I have upwards of £350 more to pay for materials and labour. The loss to me would be so serious that I shall be perfectly unable to meet it. I shall be under the necessity of calling my creditors together on account of my loss by this job, unless I have something to offer I fear that I shall be perfectly ruined. I am aware that I have no legal claim for anything besides the amount of my contract, but have some hope when the Trustees of the Church take into consideration that the absolute cost to me of the Building will be about £1,597, without calculating any profit, they will not allow me to be ruined by the undertaking."

The architect added this comment:—" I have no doubt of the amount being correct. Almost the whole of the loss is upon the stone work owing to miscalculation both of expense of labour and getting out the stone. The latter much more expensive than might reasonably be expected, the former has been executed in a superior manner to what was proposed, but the external appearance has the benefit of this. Professionally, of course, a contract should be adhered to."

On receiving this letter the Trustees agreed to pay an additional £100 to the builder, but this sum did not enable him to pay off his bills, and his creditors refusing to accept any composition he found himself in the Fleet prison to clear off his debts contracted on account of the Church.

His case was heard in November when he was declared entitled to his discharge when £9 4s. 6d., the amount at which his goods were valued, had been paid.

As these goods were his tools and the only means by which his living could be earned in the future, the Trustees agreed to pay the amount together with an additional £3 to enable him to get home, but they deducted this sum from the £100 that they had previously promised to him.

In the meantime the church had been completed, several minor details being done by other contractors, and it was consecrated by His Grace the Archbishop on September 25th, 1838, in the presence of a large congregation that included nineteen robed clergymen in attendance.

The cost of the building amounted to £1,525 1s. 7d., legal and professional charges, £202 1s. 6d., and Communion Plate, Bell and furnishings cost £181 10s. 6d., making a total figure of a little over £1,900. Towards this sum Lord and Lady Cornwallis subscribed £105, whilst £1,225 came from members of the Cleaver and King families and their friends.

The Rev. J. Boys, Vicar of Cranbrook and an original trustee hoped to secure the appointment of his curate, the Rev. Francis Curtis, as the first incumbent of the new church. The remaining four trustees did not support this nomination and the Rev. Thomas King, of Wallington, became the first Vicar. Possibly this may have influenced the Rev. J. Boys to oppose the grant of a licence for Baptisms and Marriages, on his preferment to Biddenden a further application was made and in 1843 the Archbishop authorized Baptisms and Churchings.

The church completed, it became necessary to provide a house for the incumbent, who resided temporarily at Merriecroft on the Common, an inconvenient arrangement in view of the distance from the church. Lord Cornwallis again provided a piece of land called Lisle's plat, valued by William Winch at £75 ; Whichcord and Walker of Maidstone were the architects and Henry Constable of Penshurst the builder. The vicarage was completed in August, 1843, at a total cost of £957—most of the money again being subscribed by those who had supported the building of the church.

Lady Louisa and her daughter next turned their attention to providing educational facilities for the district. These two energetic Irish ladies proceeded to canvass the whole area in order to find the number of people under 16 years of age, their final figures for the Common, Milkhouse Street and the Castle being 411 adults and 273 " minors under 16."

In the course of their canvass they noted the names of all the men they found who were unable to read, more than 30 (their activities did not apparently extend to the women).

Armed with his information, the help of Lord Cornwallis again provided a piece of land and the school was built and ready for use by 1841, at a total cost of £352—grants totalling £106 and the proceeds of a sale of work, £247, providing the necessary finance.

Other generous gifts to the village by these two ladies included a substantial contribution to the original endowment of £1,000 of the church, a gift of £110 towards necessary repairs in 1850, the presentation of the clock at a cost of £110 by Lady Louisa in 1855, and finally a legacy of £2,000 towards the augmentation of the living under the will of Mrs. Cleaver, who died at Brenchley in 1883.

Such is the mutability of human affairs, that despite all these valuable contributions for the common good of the village, the names of Lady Louisa de Spaen and Mrs. Caroline Cleaver have passed out of the memory of Sissinghurst.

It was sometime about 1850 that the name of Milkhouse Street—to Victorian ears it possibly sounded a rather common name—ceased to be used, and Sissinghurst became the official designation of the village. The earlier variant of the name, Saxinghurst, or Saxenhurst, originally a dene of Westgate, Canterbury, and owned by the Prior and Chapter of Christ Church, is, like the neighbouring Bettenham, of pre-Conquest origin, they were both settlements dating back to the 10th century or earlier. The manor, held of Christ Church, Canterbury, by knight service, dates back to the 12th century, being held by the family of Saxenhurst, one of whom, Stephen de Saxenhurst, is witness to a Charter of Cumbwell Abbey dated about 1180. Another Charter of 1255 bears the signature of Galfridus de Saxinhurst, whilst a deed relating to land at Delmonden in Cranbrook is dated 1206.

John de Saxenhurst paid relief to King Edward III in 1307, on the occasion of the marriage of the sister of the King. The manor passed by marriage to the family of Barham, who lived at Sissinghurst until the time of Henry VII, when they sold part of the property to Thomas Baker, whose grandson, John, later Sir John, bought the remainder of the estate in the early part of the 16th century.

Sir John Baker had a distinguished career, and as Recorder of London, Member of Parliament, Speaker of the House of Commons, he played an important part in public affairs during the reigns of Henry VIII, Edward VI and Mary. For the support that he gave to Queen Mary in her re-introduction of the "Old Religion" he somewhat undeservedly earned the local name of "Bloody Baker."

When Henry VIII was disposing of the lands and properties of the Religious Foundations he found a ready purchaser in Sir John Baker, who acquired the Manors of Teston, Hunton, West Farleigh, Camden and the lands of Trinity Chapel, Milkhouse, together with other properties formerly owned by Christ Church, Canterbury. He demolished the old manor house at Sissinghurst, building on the site a large residence in the new style of architecture then coming into fashion, brick being used on an extensive scale although the older form of timber framed walls filled in with plaster was employed for the rear of the premises. The entrance lead into a coutyard from which one passed under the towers to enter the inner courtyard around which the more important rooms were grouped. Although most of this imposing house has been demolished, the entrance gateway and the two towers over the central arch have been spared this fate and remain as beautiful examples of early Tudor brickwork.

Sir John Baker died in 1558, being succeeded by his son, Richard, who had the honour of entertaining Queen Elizabeth I during her progress of Kent in 1573, being knighted by the Queen on this occasion.

The Bakers continued to reside at Sissinghurst for more than two hundred years, always taking an active interest in the affairs of the parish until the death of the last Sir John in 1661, leaving three daughters as his coheirs. Lady Baker lived at Sissinghurst until she died in 1691, and soon after this date the family ceased to occupy the house. The property was later mortgaged to Sir Horace Mann, of Linton, and early in the 18th century is passed to him by sale. Horace Walpole visited Sissinghurst in 1752 and his often quoted description bears repetition:—"Yesterday after twenty mishaps we got to Sissinghurst to dinner. There is a park in ruins and a house in ten time greater ruin. You go through an arch of stables to the house, the court of which is perfect and very beautiful. It has a good appartment and a fine gallery 120 ft. long by 18 ft., which takes up one side. The wainscot is pretty and entire, the ceiling vaulted and painted. The whole is built for show, for the back of the house is lath and plaster." This last observation is less than just to the timber framed and plaster walls that have been shown to be as durable as brick in many of the old houses in Cranbrook.

Such was the condition of Sissinghurst when it was leased by the Government in 1756 for the accommodation of the ever increasing number of prisoners of war following the outbreak of the Seven Years War. It was from this time that it came to be called " The Castle." The prisoners were all seamen taken from the numerous prizes captured by the Navy ; they slept in hammocks, each with a flock bed, a blanket and a coverlet.

Conditions were hard and discipline severe in a prisoner of war camp. Public subscriptions were opened for the relief of prisoners in this country. A letter of thanks from the men confined at Sissinghurst contains excuses for some who had sold the clothes supplied to them by this means in order to obtain urgent necessities such as tobacco, postage for letters, and paying for a remission of their punishment when placed on half rations.

Officers were placed on parole and allowed to live in the town, there is a letter signed by 27 of the paroled naval officers in which they complain that they were not allowed by the one mile limit of their parole to visit their crews confined at Sissinghurst Castle—two miles away—" to help them in their distress and to prevent them being robbed by the English who have the monopoly of getting things for sale into the prison, notably the jailer and canteen man."

An earlier letter—in 1756—from officers on parole at Cranbrook, prayed to be sent to Maidstone on the plea that there was no lodging to be had in Cranbrook except at exhorbitant rates ; the bakers only baked once or twice a week ; that vegetables were hardly to be obtained, and that finally they were ill-treated by the inhabitants.

By contrast, a petition from 37 officers at Goudhurst is accompanied by a testimony signed by several parishioners which commences : " We the inhabitants of the parish of Goudhurst certify that we never was insulted in any respect by the French gentlemen nor to their knowledge have they caused any riot . . . ."

The governor of the camp, a certain Mr. Cook, appears to have been unduly severe, and the sentries were disposed to use their muskets freely. Ferdinand Brehost was shot dead by a sentry in 1757 and a short time after Jacob Loppe was shot dead in his hammock by a sentry, who thought that they were showing a light, but it transpired that it was the reflection of a lamp outside the building.

On another occasion two prisoners were shot by a sentry who was afterwards found to be out of his senses. In 1760 several prisoners made an attempt to escape through a drain to the moat, they had been successful in passing two of the three sentries but were challenged by the third. Realising that there was no hope of escape they called out, " Don't fire, we surrender," but despite this the sentry did fire at point blank range, killing one of the prisoners.

A few weeks after this incident the good people of Cranbrook were sent flying out of church one Sunday morning by the rumour that 1,000 prisoners had broken out of Sissinghurst, but happily it proved to be a false alarm.

The prisoners petitioned the Admiralty for some alleviation of their hardships, whilst the French Minister at The Hague handed to our Ambassador there a protest complaining of the inhuman treatment of the prisoners at Sissinghurst by Mr. Cook.

The Admiralty ordered an enquiry to be made and the Commissioner reported that although exaggerated, there was too much reason for the complaints, although the enormities complained of had been committed by the common sentinels—" the lowest of the people." The officers had promised to stop such irregular conduct for the future.

A change in the governor followed and from then until the prisoners were repatriated in 1763, conditions were much better and there were few complaints.

During the period that the prisoners were held at the Castle, a permanent garrison was maintained in Cranbrook for guard purposes. The officers not on duty at Sissinghurst were billeted at " The George." The quarters for the men were in the row of cottages on Milkhouse Heath now occupied by Camden Lodge and at Barracks Farm, a name derived from this time.

Edward Gibbon, the historian, while serving in the Hampshire Militia, undertook a short tour of duty at Cranbrook, and his journal shows that he did not like either the town or the duty that brought him here. " Dec. 12, 1760. I relieved the guard at Sissinghurst, a strong large old seat situated in the middle of a park and containing about 1,750 prisoners. The duty was hard, the dirt most oppressive thro' which the men from their wretched barracks had two miles to march every day, and the officers three from a county town almost as miserable. The inconceivable dirtiness of the season, the country and the spot aggravated the hardships of a duty too heavy for our numbers."

Neither Gibbon nor the French officers present Cranbrook in a very favourable light, their views were no doubt prejudiced although there is every reason to suppose that the bad condition of the roads, also mentioned by Horace Walpole, does present an accurate picture of communications in the Weald before the Turnpike roads were constructed.

After the withdrawal of the French prisoners the Castle remained uninhabited for many years, the bad state of repair in which it was left received no attention until 1796, when the Parish of Cranbrook decided to lease the house and land as a workhouse. The derelict buildings were put into some sort of order and for the next forty years were used to house the sick, poor, and aged of the parish until the new Union workhouse was built at Hartley in 1836. The 300 or more acres of land attached to the Castle were farmed by Trustees, and employed those able-bodied men who could otherwise have been a charge on the Poor Rate, the lease not being finally surrendered until 1856.

When the buildings were given up in 1836 they had fallen into such a serious condition of decay and disrepair that it was decided that they must be pulled down, and so this "magnificent pile," as it had been termed, vanished except for the towers and the parts flanking the main gateway. Much of the material may have been used in making up the new road built about this period which gave access to the village, in place of the old route by the Horse Race on to the Common.

The ruins of the Castle were bought in 1930 by the Hon. Lady Nicolson (Miss V. Sackville-West), a direct descendant of Sir John Baker, whose daughter married the Elizabethan poet and statesman, Sir Thomas Sackville, Lord Buckhurst and First Earl of Dorset. Much care and thought have since been devoted to the restoration and preservation of the surviving building, whilst the gardens that have grown up around them are amongst the most beautiful in the county, open daily to the public, as are the gardens at Sissinghurst Place, for 250 years the home of the Plummers, and later occupied by Lady Louisa de Spaen and Mrs. Cleaver.